The Leader in
Field Guide

Aligning **Academics**

Name

 FranklinCovey. | EDUCATION

IMPORTANT NOTICE

ABOUT FRANKLINCOVEY EDUCATION

For nearly three decades, FranklinCovey Education, a division of FranklinCovey, has been one of the world's most prominent and trusted providers of educational leadership programs and transformational processes. Our mission is to enable greatness in students, teachers, and schools everywhere. The FranklinCovey Education team is primarily composed of outstanding former teachers and administrators from various educational levels and entities. Franklin Covey Co. (NYSE: FC) is a global, public company specializing in performance improvement. We help organizations and individuals achieve results that require a change in human behavior. Our expertise is in seven areas: leadership, execution, productivity, trust, sales performance, customer loyalty, and education.

These terms are registered trademarks of FranklinCovey:
Habit 1: Be Proactive®
Habit 2: Begin With the End in Mind®
Habit 3: Put First Things First®
Habit 4: Think Win-Win®
Habit 5: Seek First to Understand, Then to Be Understood®
Habit 6: Synergize®
Habit 7: Sharpen the Saw®
The 8th Habit®: Find Your Voice and Inspire Others to Find Theirs

Table of Contents

Building Momentum 1

    Celebrating and Thinking Ahead

    Remembering the Why

    Reaching New Heights

Achieving Personal WIGs 19

    The 4 Disciplines

    Gallery of Personal WIGs

    Setting a Personal WIG

Achieving Team (Class) WIGs 49

    The 4 Disciplines in Teams

    Gallery of Team (Class) WIGs

    Setting a Team (Class) WIG

Achieving Student WIGs 81

    The 4 Disciplines With Students

    Gallery of Student WIGs

    Setting a Student WIG

    Leadership Notebooks

    Student-Led Conferences

Wrapping Up 143

    Putting It All Together

    Designing an Implementation Plan

Appendix 155

    Self-Assessing the 7 Habits

Building Momentum

- Celebrating and Thinking Ahead
- Remembering the Why
- Reaching New Heights

Building Momentum

Welcome back!

The Leader in Me enables staff members, students, and families to increase their effectiveness through the daily application of timeless leadership principles. You are an important part of the process.

This Field Guide is designed to build upon the momentum you have already generated as a school and as an individual. It is the third in a series of three:

1. Launching **Leadership**

2. Creating **Culture**

3. Aligning **Academics**

Each Field Guide focuses on one of three universal challenges all schools face: leadership, culture, and academics. This particular guide emphasizes academics. Though *The Leader in Me* is not a reading, math, science, or other academic subject-based process, it applies key leadership principles and skills to academics in a way that is intended to increase students' ownership for their learning, help them to work more effectively in teams, and see themselves as lifelong learners.

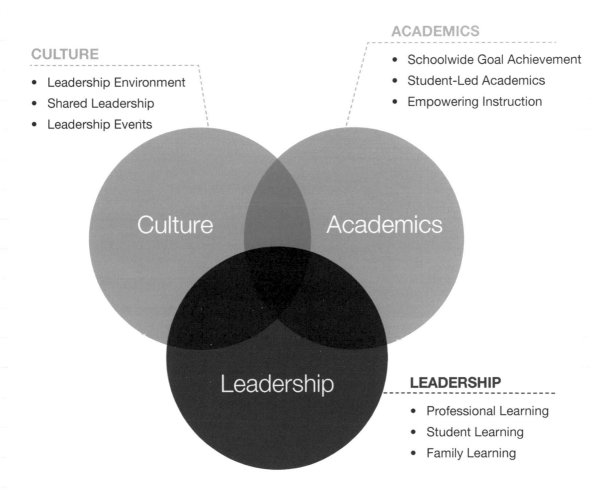

CULTURE

- Leadership Environment
- Shared Leadership
- Leadership Events

ACADEMICS

- Schoolwide Goal Achievement
- Student-Led Academics
- Empowering Instruction

LEADERSHIP

- Professional Learning
- Student Learning
- Family Learning

Celebrating and Thinking Ahead

Sometimes looking back in time helps people to better see ahead. So pause on occasion, and reflect on the progress your school has made in its journey with *The Leader in Me*. What has gone well? What can be improved? Chances are that your school's greatest successes and opportunities for improvement fall within the following categories:

LEADERSHIP

Staff Learning
- Existing staff members being trained in *7 Habits/TLIM.*
- New staff members being trained in *7 Habits/TLIM.*
- The principal (and other administrators) modeling the 7 Habits for staff.

Student Learning
- Students being taught the 7 Habits using direct lessons.
- Teachers integrating the 7 Habits into core subject lessons.
- Staff modeling the 7 Habits for students.

Family Learning
- Communication about the 7 Habits and *TLIM* going home.
- Staff informing families of the 7 Habits.
- Students teaching the 7 Habits at home.

CULTURE

Leadership Environment
- The physical environment being inspiring. (What you *see*.)
- The language of leadership being spoken. (What you *hear*.)
- The emotional environment. (What you *feel*.)

Shared Leadership
- Students being given opportunities to be leaders.
- Students' opinions being valued and utilized.
- Students finding their voice.

Leadership Events
- Schoolwide events reinforcing leadership.
- Classroom events reinforcing leadership.
- Family & Community events highlighting leadership.

 **DISCUSSION**
Plus/Delta on Leadership and Culture

Use a Plus/Delta Chart to celebrate the school's achievements (pluses +) in implementing *The Leader in Me* to this point, and identify things you might change (deltas Δ) in moving ahead. Use the descriptions of leadership and culture on the previous page to prompt your thinking.

Δ—The Greek symbol delta is used to refer to change that happens over a certain time interval.

Remembering the Why

The Leader in Me is a journey, not a destination. As with any journey, it is far more likely to be done with vigor when people are:

- Highly effective as INDIVIDUALS.
- Working together as a TEAM.
- In pursuit of a compelling PURPOSE—a meaningful why.

The lack of oxygen above 8,000 meters can be fatal to climbers.

SUMMIT / 8,848 METERS

CAMP 4 / 8,000 METERS

CAMP 3 / 7,162 METERS

CAMP 2—CULTURE

CAMP 1—LEADERSHIP

BASE CAMP / 5,334 METERS

No other mountain on earth has a higher altitude than Mount Everest. Its peak rise 8,850 meters (29,035 feet) above sea leve

© Franklin Covey Co.

*Paradigm - way you see something

BUILDING MOMENTUM

VIDEO

Everest

Compare your *Leader in Me* journey with the journey of this team of climbers.

What qualities do INDIVIDUALS on the team exhibit?

- put others first
- compassion
- communication (team meetings)
- perserverance

What leadership principles does the TEAM exhibit?

- strong foundation of trust

What was the compelling PURPOSE, or *why*, of the climbing team?

- help Erik get himself to the top

leadership can come from an unexpected place

> "I think everyone has a yearning for greatness inside them—that ability to reach out into uncertainty and in a sense, I guess, to climb blind."
>
> ERIK WEIHENMAYER

DISCUSSION
The Why at Your School

In small teams, discuss what you feel are the main purposes of doing *The Leader in Me* at your school.

For Students

For Staff Members

For You

The Why Beneath *The Leader in Me*

The Leader In Me enables individuals to become more independent (Private Victory®) and more interdependent (Public Victory®) and to utilize those strengths to make a more meaningful contribution (find their voice) at school, at home, and in the communities in which they reside.

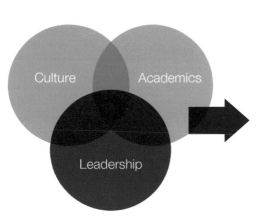

To enable people to be more:

- Independent.
- Interdependent.
- Able to make a meaningful contribution.

MEANS (THE *HOW*)   **ENDS (THE *WHY*)**

Reaching New Heights

As with any journey, momentum is built by achieving new milestones. People want to feel a sense of progress—students and adults.

There are two general ways to take *The Leader in Me* to new heights:

 Widen and deepen the application of the leadership paradigms and principles already discussed in previous Field Guides. For example, the concepts embedded in the Core Paradigms as well as The 7 Habits of Highly Effective People can be applied more deeply or broadly across the school.

CORE PARADIGMS

The following paradigms are core to *The Leader in Me*, as compared to "common paradigms" held in many schools and classrooms.

COMMON PARADIGMS	THE LEADER IN ME PARADIGMS
Leadership is for the few.	Everyone can be a leader.
A few people are gifted.	Everyone has genius.
To improve schools, the system needs to change first.	Change starts with me.
Educators control and direct student learning.	Educators empower students to lead their own learning.
Focus solely on academic achievement.	Develop the whole person.

THE 7 HABITS OF HIGHLY EFFECTIVE PEOPLE®

Dr. Stephen R. Covey's highly acclaimed *The 7 Habits of Highly Effective People* has aided leaders around the globe in achieving their highest priorities. The same habits can be applied to academics.

HABIT	BASIC DEFINITIONS	HIGHLY EFFECTIVE PRACTICES
1. Be Proactive	You're in Charge	• Pause and respond based on principles and desired results. • Use proactive language. • Focus on your Circle of Influence®. • Become a Transition Person.
2. Begin With the End in Mind	Have a Plan	• Define outcomes before you act. • Create a Personal Mission Statement.
3. Put First Things First	Work First, Then Play	• Focus on your highest priories. • Eliminate the unimportant. • Plan every week. • Stay true in the moment of choice.
4. Think Win-Win	Everyone Can Win	• Build your Emotional Bank Account with others. • Have an Abundance Mentality. • Balance courage and consideration. • Consider other people's wins as well as your own. • Create Win-Win Agreements.
5. Seek First to Understand, Then to Be Understood	Listen Before You Talk	• Practice Empathetic Listening. • Respectfully seek to be understood.
6. Synergize	Together Is Better	• Value differences. • Seek 3rd Alternatives.
7. Sharpen the Saw	Balance Feels Best	• Achieve the Daily Private Victory in four areas: body, heart, mind, and spirit.

Like climbing Everest, The Leader in Me journey takes people to higher levels one step at a time.

ACTIVITY
To New Heights... and Beyond

Think of your role and work area. On the spectrums below, put an X in <u>each</u> of the camps that you feel you have achieved. Then write on the line one thing you can do to reach a new height in the particular area of focus.

LEADERSHIP

Professional Learning

BASE CAMP	CAMP 1	CAMP 2	CAMP 3	CAMP 4
I just arrived at base camp.	I consistently grow my knowledge of the 7 Habits and other *TLIM* content.	I share *TLIM* and 7 Habits ideas with colleagues.	I mentor new staff members in *TLIM*.	People see me as a role model of the 7 Habits.

One thing:_____

Student Learning

BASE CAMP	CAMP 1	CAMP 2	CAMP 3	CAMP 4
I have not taught the 7 Habits to students.	I do a good job of teaching students the 7 Habits with their key concepts.	I integrate the 7 Habits and other leadership principles into everyday talk and/or lessons.	I use the 7 Habits and other leadership principles to solve challenges with students.	I utilize students to teach the 7 Habits to other students.

One thing:_____

Family Learning

BASE CAMP	CAMP 1	CAMP 2	CAMP 3	CAMP 4
I have not taught the 7 Habits to families.	I send periodic notes home to parents that have leadership quotes or thoughts on them.	I assign periodic 7 Habits homework for students to do with parents.	I involve parents in teaching students about leadership.	My home is a *Leader in Me*-type of home.

One thing:_____

CULTURE

Leadership Environment

BASE CAMP	CAMP 1	CAMP 2	CAMP 3	CAMP 4
My work-area walls have nothing about leadership on them.	I have put up posters of the 7 Habits for students to see.	My work-area walls inspire students to learn and be leaders.	Students have filled the walls with their work and leadership messages.	I communicate to students their worth and potential daily.

One thing:_____

Shared Leadership

BASE CAMP	CAMP 1	CAMP 2	CAMP 3	CAMP 4
I do everything myself.	I give students responsibilities so they feel needed.	I give students leadership roles to help them develop skills.	I give students "choice and voice" in identifying the leadership roles they fill.	I help students find their voice.

One thing:_____

Leadership Events

BASE CAMP	CAMP 1	CAMP 2	CAMP 3	CAMP 4
I attend team and school events when asked.	My team/class meets weekly to talk about plans and goals.	My team/class discusses leadership principles like the 7 Habit during meetings.	I involve students in planning and leading events.	I involve parents and community leaders in teaching about leadership.

One thing:_____

Learn and apply new leadership principles. The second general way to take *The Leader in Me* to new heights is to learn additional leadership principles and apply them. In addition to the 7 Habits and the five Core Paradigms, this Field Guide introduces new leadership principles and skills that are discovered in *The 4 Disciplines of Execution*.

THE 4 DISCIPLINES OF EXECUTION®

The 4 Disciplines have their origins in a proven methodology that has been formed after working with literally thousand of leaders of organizations and teams around the globe. They enable organizations, teams, and individuals to achieve their highest priorities and goals.

The remaining portion of this Field Guide will apply the 4 Disciplines to:

- Staff members (Achieving Personal WIGs).

- Teams, particularly classrooms (Achieving Team WIGs).

- Students (Achieving Student WIGs).

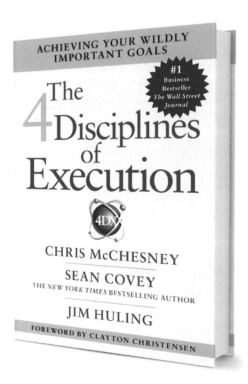

Notes

WIGs - Wildly Important goals

Notes

PERSONA
VICTORII

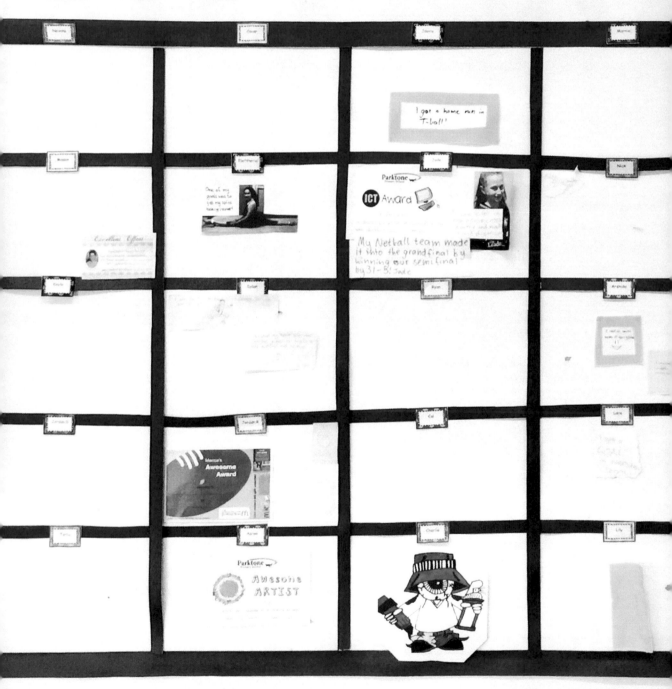

I got a home run in T-ball!

Parktone
ICT Award

My Netball team made it into the grand final by winning our semi final by 31-8. Jade

Excellent Effort

Mentor's
Awesome
Award

Parktone
AWESOME
ARTIST

Achieving Personal WIGs

- The 4 Disciplines
- Gallery of Personal WIGs
- Setting a Personal WIG

Achieving Personal WIGs

Most people spend their days and minutes living in one of three territories:

WASTELAND: Doing tasks that are *not important*.

WHIRLWIND: Doing many *important* tasks that keep them busy, busy.

WILDLY IMPORTANT: Focused on one or two *most important* priorities.

Relatively few people choose to live their life in the "wasteland," so it is far more likely to find them caught up in the "whirlwind." Yet, what is clear is that some whirlwind tasks and goals are more important than others. We call them "wildly important." If we are not disciplined in how we use our time, we allow lesser important goals to keep us from achieving that which is of greatest importance.

What is a **Wildly Important Goal**?

Failure to achieve this goal renders any other achievements inconsequential.

My goal is to increase working out 2 – 3 times a week to 4 – 5 times a week.
- Mrs. Bryant

At Brookview Everyone Has Goals

The designed outcomes for this section of the guide are:

- To enable you to become a more effective contributor to the school by focusing on what is most important.

- To have you learn a four-step process for achieving goals that can be applied to many aspects of life.

- To empower you to model the process for students.

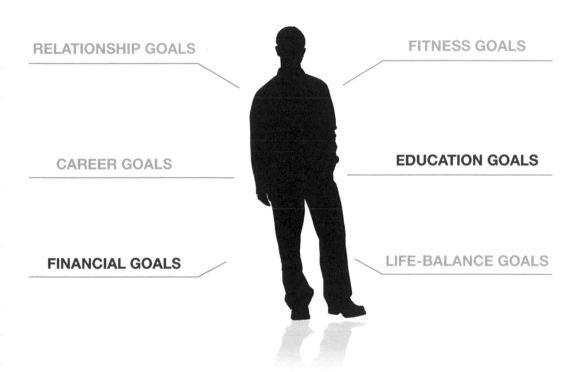

RELATIONSHIP GOALS

FITNESS GOALS

CAREER GOALS

EDUCATION GOALS

FINANCIAL GOALS

LIFE-BALANCE GOALS

"Ever since I went blind, it's been a dream in the back of my mind to climb the world's tallest peak.... I needed to figure out a way to find a pattern through that icefall, to find some systems that work for me.... Sometimes you have to rise to the occasion—right now you gotta be good and execute right now, every step of the way."

ERIK WEIHENMAYER

The 4 Disciplines

Many people are good at "setting" goals; far fewer are effective at "achieving" goals. The 4 Disciplines form a tested, sequential process that helps individuals and teams achieve their Wildly Important Goals. Embedded in the process are valuable principles and tools for decision making, problem solving, critical thinking, and being more effective.

So, what are the 4 Disciplines?

DISCIPLINE 1: Focus on the Wildly Important

DISCIPLINE 2: Act on the Lead Measures

DISCIPLINE 3: Keep a Compelling Scoreboard

DISCIPLINE 4: Create a Cadence of Accountability

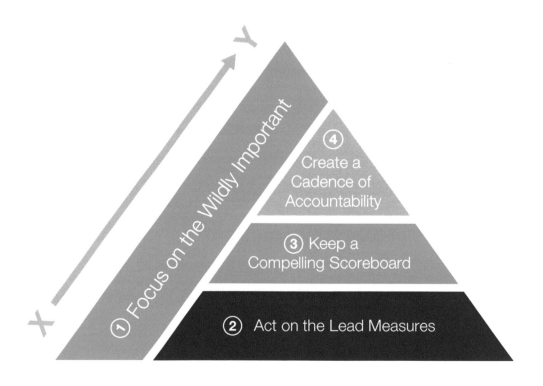

 **VIDEO**
The 4 Disciplines

Capture the main ideas of each of the 4 Disciplines and be prepared to reteach one or more of the disciplines to one or more peers.

Discipline 1: Focus on the Wildly Important

Discipline 2: Act on the Lead Measures

Discipline 3: Keep a Compelling Scoreboard

Discipline 4: Create a Cadence of Accountability

> "Two requirements for sustainable change:
> 1. We need to know where we really want to go.
> 2. We need to have a very clear picture of where are we really."
>
> **PETER SENGE,** *THE FIFTH DISCIPLINE*

Discipline 1: Focus on the Wildly Important

KEY PRINCIPLE: FOCUS

 BRAINSTORM A LIST OF WILDLY IMPORTANT GOALS.

Brainstorm a list of ideas that immediately come to mind when asking yourself the question:

"What is the one area of my life where change will have the greatest impact?"

Personal WIGs should align with your Personal Mission Statement and fall within your Circle of Influence. It may help to begin brainstorming by considering four important areas: your physical well-being, your social/emotional well-being, your mental growth, and any unique contributions you want to make.

 NARROW THE LIST TO ONE PERSONAL WIG.

There will always be more good ideas for WIGs than there is capacity to implement them. So focus on one or two Wildly Important Goals, then consistently invest your time and energy into achieving them. It may mean saying no to some *great* ideas, at least for now.

In identifying your WIG, state it in a positive sentence that includes *why* it is important.

EXAMPLE: *I will lose five pounds so that I will feel more energetic in doing my work.*

 Fundamental Rule:
Do not set a personal WIG that is dependent upon others to change their behavior.

3   **WRITE THE WIG IN A "FROM X TO Y BY WHEN" FORMAT.**

Goals are most useful when written in specific, realistic terms that include:

X = Where are you now? The "Starting Line."

Y = Where do you want to be? The "Finish Line."

When = Over what period of time will the WIG be spread? The "Deadline."

EXAMPLE: *I will go from 150 pounds to 145 pounds by May 5.*

TIP: The "when" should be far enough out to have time to meet the goal, yet close enough to keep it at the main center of focus.

4   **POST THE WIG IN A VISIBLE LOCATION.**

Placing your WIG in a visible location keeps what's most important at the forefront. Note, however, that 80 percent of your energy will still be directed at maintaining the "whirlwind." So don't worry that by making one or two goals most important you will ignore everything else.

It takes more than being SMART to "achieve" a goal. It takes discipline.

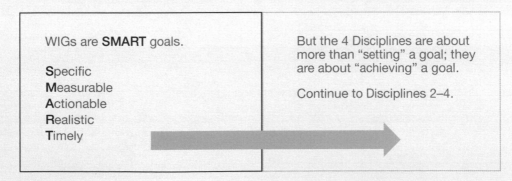

WIGs are **SMART** goals.

Specific
Measurable
Actionable
Realistic
Timely

But the 4 Disciplines are about more than "setting" a goal; they are about "achieving" a goal.

Continue to Disciplines 2–4.

Discipline 2: Act on the Lead Measures

KEY PRINCIPLE: LEVERAGE

IDENTIFY A LIST OF POTENTIAL STRATEGIES FOR ACHIEVING YOUR WIG.

List specific strategies or changes of behavior that will "lead" to the goal being achieved. They should be something you can *influence* and be *predictive* of you ultimately achieving the goal. Be realistic. You can always make adjustments at a later point.

EXAMPLES:

- *Do 30 minutes of brisk walking before dinner each evening.*

- *Get a pedometer and do a minimum of 10,000 steps five days a week.*

- *Drink five tall glasses of water daily.*

SELECT THE ONE OR TWO STRATEGIES THAT HAVE THE HIGHEST LEVERAGE.

Identify the one or two strategies or changes in behavior that have the greatest potential to impact your chances of achieving your WIG. In a real sense, you are saying, "I am making a strategic bet that if I do these two things, my likelihood of achieving the goal will go way up." Factors to consider include:

- What best practices have others implemented to achieve the same (or a similar) goal?

- If you have data, what are the greatest gaps that need to be closed?

- What barriers may interfere with progress?

TIP: In some cases, the best strategy is to focus on the one singular action step (instead of many) that will have the greatest impact.

TURN THE HIGHEST-LEVERAGED STRATEGIES INTO LEAD MEASURES.

Many people make the mistake of only measuring the outcomes they are striving to achieve—their Y; or in this example, their weight. However, successful goal achievers track most closely their progress on how often they complete their key strategies or action steps. The measures used to track the highest-leveraged strategies are known as lead measures. So if your goal is to lose 5 pounds, then potential lead measures might be:

Lead Measure 1

Take 10,000 steps five days a week.

WIG ("From X to Y by When")

Lose 5 pounds by 5/5.

Lead Measure 2

Drink five tall glasses of water daily.

 TAKE DIRECT ACTION ON YOUR LEAD MEASURES.

This is where deep discipline is required. Well-written goals and accurate measures are of little worth unless the lead measures are acted upon.

ACHIEVING PERSONAL WIGS

Key INSIGHT: There are two types of WIGs and action steps.

WIG	Project-Based	Behavior-Based
	EXAMPLE: *Build a library so students can access books.*	EXAMPLE: *Stop bullying so students can focus on learning.*
LEAD MEASURES (STRATEGIES)	Make a timeline, Flow Chart, or Gantt Chart. Track progress regularly.	Narrow to two and track them daily (at least frequently).

Discipline 3: Keep a Compelling Scoreboard

KEY PRINCIPLE: ENGAGEMENT

 CREATE A SCOREBOARD.

People behave differently when they are keeping score. Effective scoreboards display:

1. Lead Measures: This shows if you are actually completing the strategies and action steps as often as each day.

   EXAMPLE: *Check off on a monthly calendar if you drank five tall glasses of water each day.*

2. Lag Measures: This shows where you "are" in your progress relative to the actual goal (Y).

   EXAMPLE: *Display how much you weigh at the start, after Week 1, after Week 2, and so forth.*

3. Goal Line: A powerful motivator is to create a "goal" line to beat. It shows where you want to be at various milestones and gives you a target to conquer. It creates a "Game on!" mindset that quickly allows you to see if you are winning or losing.

   EXAMPLE: *If you want to lose five pounds in five weeks, the trend line to beat would display the loss of one pound every week.*

GIVE THE SCOREBOARD THE "COMPELLING" TEST.

Scoreboards that are complicated or show too much data can be more confusing and discouraging than compelling. Characteristics of a compelling scoreboard include:

1. Contains both desired outcomes (Y) and lead measures.

2. Is simple; in five seconds or less, you can tell if you are "winning."

3. Shows progress.

4. Is fun and engaging.

 TIP: The most engaging factor in a compelling scoreboard is if it shows progress. People like to see that they are progressing on a consistent (even weekly) basis. Call them "small wins," "baby steps," or whatever; adults and students like the feel of achievement.

 PLACE THE SCOREBOARD IN A VISIBLE LOCATION AND UPDATE IT OFTEN.

Results drive people to be engaged. When people see positive results happening from their efforts, they become more engaged. So put the scoreboard in a highly visible place where they can see it and then work hard to make it show progress. The scoreboard location should allow you to easily update and track progress.

ACHIEVING PERSONAL WIGS

Discipline 4: Create a Cadence of Accountability

KEY PRINCIPLE: ACCOUNTABILITY

 SELECT AN ACCOUNTABILITY PARTNER.

When people have a partner to account to—someone they trust—they are far more likely to achieve a goal. So in pursuing your WIG, seek out an Accountability Partner who has **TACT**:

Trust. Are they on your side? Will they hold a confidence?

Availability. Can they meet at times convenient with your schedule?

Courage. Will they challenge you to new heights in a positive way?

Talent. Do they have strengths that can elevate your thinking and skills?

What Is the Probability of Achieving Your Goal?

Hear an idea you like.	10%
Consciously decide to adopt an idea.	25%
Decide when you will do it.	40%
Plan when you will do it.	50%
Commit to someone else that you will do it.	65%
Have a specific appointment with the person you commit to, at which time you report to him or her whether you have done it and make new commitments.	95%

MEET AT A CONSISTENT, DESIGNATED TIME.

Set a time to meet on a steady basis—preferably once a week or more, and at a consistent time. Keep the meetings (called "WIG Sessions") short and focused. While WIG Sessions might vary in content, the agenda remains consistent:

1. Report on previous commitments.

2. Review and update the scoreboard.

3. Make new commitments.

 TIP: Each new commitment should meet two standards: First, the commitment must represent a specific deliverable; and second, the commitment must influence the lead measures.

ADJUST AS NECESSARY.

Occasionally, the original WIG or lead measures may need to be adjusted. WIGs should be challenging enough to be motivational, yet achievable enough to be attainable. Make sure your measuring stick is the appropriate length for your needs. Learn from successes and failures.

CELEBRATE MILESTONES, NOT JUST THE FINISH LINE.

Intrinsic rewards have more meaning and last longer than extrinsic rewards. Though extrinsic rewards can be very motivating to students (and even adults), they must be attached to an intrinsic reward to have full and lasting value.

Gallery of Personal WIGs

This section of the guide introduces you to samples of personal WIGs and scoreboards others have created and pursued. Ask yourself:

- What do I like about them?

- Do any of the goals apply to me?

- What would I do differently?

Use the ideas and any others you come up with to begin thinking about a personal WIG you will pursue. Think particularly of WIGs you would be willing to share with others, including students.

VIDEO
Personal WIGs

This video shares insights from three educators on how they applied the
4 Disciplines in pursuing personal WIGs. Look for:

What are their "From X to Y by When" goals?

What are their lead measures?

What types of scoreboards do they use?

Who are their accountability partners? How often do they meet?

What is the "end in mind"? I NEED MORE ENERGY IN THE AFTERNOON.

165 POUNDS	160 POUNDS	5 WEEKS (MAR 20)
Where I am now.	Where I want to be.	By when?

ACT ON THE LEAD MEASURES

What action steps are needed to achieve the WIG? (Star the Leads)

- INSTEAD OF DRINKING SODA, I WILL DRINK 5 LARGE GLASSES OF WATER PER DAY.

- I WILL WALK 50 MINUTES 4 DAYS EACH WEEK.

CREATE A CADENCE OF ACCOUNTABILITY

My accountability partner(s) is:

MY STUDENTS

When and where we will meet is:

EVERY FRIDAY DURING "TEAM" TIME

How we will celebrate is:

I'LL FEEL BETTER & REWARD THE STUDENTS FOR HELPING ME.

MONTH	JANUARY					
Sunday	Monday	Tuesday	Wednesday	Thursday	Friday	Saturday
		1	2	3	4	5
6	7	8	9	10	11	12
13	14	15	16	17	18	19
20	21	22	23	24	25	26
27	28	29	30	31		

● 5 CUPS WATER PER DAY
● 50 MINUTES WALKING 4 TIMES PER WEEK

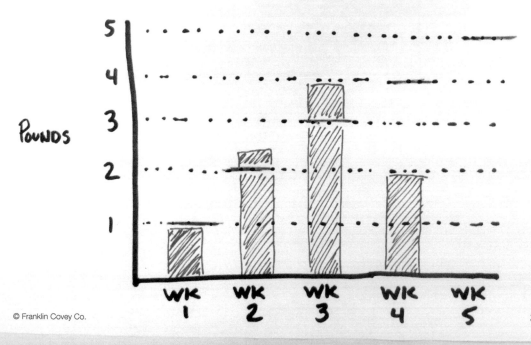

POUNDS

WK 1   WK 2   WK 3   WK 4   WK 5

FOCUS ON THE WILDLY IMPORTANT

What is the "end in mind"? Read two highly recommended books
to improve how I teach math.

O

books read on math
skills in 7 years.

Where I am now.

2

books read

Where I want to be.

End of
November

By when.

ACT ON THE LEAD MEASURES

What action steps are needed to achieve the WIG?

One book is 263 pages, the other 227 pages. Total 490.
Must average 5 pages per day.

Teach my grade-level team what I learn
once each week.

CREATE A CADENCE OF ACCOUNTABILITY

My accountability partner(s) is:

Grade-level team

When and where we will meet is

Friday's during team meeting.

How we will celebrate is:

Student share my accomplishment
on morning announcement.

5 pages per day

5	10	15	20	25	30	35	40	45	50
55	60	65	70	75	80	85	90	95	100
105	110	115	120	125	130	135	140	145	150
155	160	165	170	175	180	185	190	195	200
205	210	220	225	230	235	240	245	250	255
260	263								

5	10	15	20	25	30	35	40	45	50
55	60	65	70	75	80	85	90	95	100
105	110	115	120	125	130	135	140	145	150
155	160	165	170	175	180	185	190	195	200
205	210	220	225	227					

Teaching to Team

X Week 1	X Week 6	___ Week 11
X Week 2	X Week 7	___ Week 12
___ Week 3	___ Week 8	___ Week 13
X Week 4	___ Week 9	___ Week 14
___ Week 5	___ Week 10	

Book 1   Book 2

finished Oct 28

Name: Mrs. Wilson

Accountability Partner: Mr. Gammouh

Goal:

I will take 10,000 steps per day, 5 days a week, for the month of September.

Strategies:

- Walk for 20 minutes each day (put it in my schedule)
- Stay active with my kids (biking, soccer, etc.)
- Track on fitbit app

September 2015

Sun	Mon	Tue	Wed	Thu	Fri	Sat
		1	2 ✓	3	4 ✓	5
6 ✓	7	8 ✓	9 ✓	10 ✓	11 ✓	12 ✓
13 ✓	14 ✓	15	16 ✓	17 ✓	18 ✓	19 ✓
20 ✓	21 ✓	22	23 ✓	24 ✓	25 ✓	26 ✓
27	28 ✓	29	30			

Wow! You are working hard to get those steps :)

Name: Mrs. Vernengo

Accountability Partner: Ms. McGillivray

Goal:

I will go to bed by 9:00 P.M. 5 nights a week during the school year.

Strategies:

- No technology after 8:00 P.M.
- Read a book at 8:30 P.M.
- Lights out at 9:00 P.M.

September 2015

Sun	Mon	Tue	Wed	Thu	Fri	Sat
		1 ✗	2 ✗	3 ✗	4	5
6	7 ✗	8 ✗	9	10 ✗	11	12
13 ✗	14 ✗	15	16 ✗	17 ✗	18	19
20 ✗	21 ✗	22	23	24	25	26
27 ✗	28	29	30			

38

This was a great week! You can do it

Mrs. Swenson
108 Warrior Way
Music

My goal is...

Read at least 1 book
a month for 5 months.

Action steps:
Read 20 min or more
6 days a week

Current book:
Drumming to
the Beat of
Different
Marchers
By Debbie Silver

JANUARY 2015

	Tuesday	Wednesday	Thursday	Friday	Saturday
			1 75min	2 60min	3 60min Redbird Christmas Complete
4 25min	5 20	6 30	7 20	8 20	9 O	10 10
11 30	12 30	13 O	14 30	15 20 10 Habits of Happy Mothers	16 20	17 O
18 O	19 40	20 20	21 O	22 20	23 O	24 O
25 20	26 O	27	28	29	30	31

January Books Read:
A Redbird Christmas
by Fannie Flagg
10 Habits of Happy
Mothers
by Meg Meeker, M.D.

My goal is...
to increase meaningful time
with my family by March 1 2015.
Action steps:
1. Phone off from 4-8 pm
   4 nights a week.
2. Have a date night with Jeff
   or Harper 1x per month.

☆=Met weekly
X=Oops!
☺ = yes

JANUARY 2015

Sunday	Monday	Tuesday	Wednesday	Thursday	Friday	Saturday
				1	2	3
4	5 X	6 X	7 ☺	8 ☺	9 ☺	10 ☺
11	12 ☺	13 ☺	14 ☺	15 ☺	16 X	17 X
18 ☺	19 ☺	20 ☺	21 ☺	22 ☺	23 X	24 X
25 ☺	26 X	27	28	29	30	31

From November to May, I
will continue to eat
healthy foods during the
week.

39

Setting a Personal WIG

One way to identify a personal WIG is to think in terms of your greatest challenges. Personal challenges come in many forms, many of which fall under leadership, culture, and academics. Some examples include:

LEADERSHIP

- I want to mentor one of the new staff members in *The Leader in Me* this year.

- I need more energy during the day.

- I want to involve parents more with *The Leader in Me*.

- I need to more frequently integrate the 7 Habits into lesson plans.

CULTURE

- I need to "let go" a bit more in my leadership style—turn more over to students.

- I want to listen more to students' opinions.

- I want to give more students a chance to fill meaningful leadership roles.

- I need to make my class meetings more effective this year.

ACADEMICS

- I need to get to know my students better so I can teach them more effectively.

- I want to improve my skills in teaching students how to read.

- I want to make my subject lessons more participative and experiential.

- I want to pursue a master's degree to increase my knowledge (and pay).

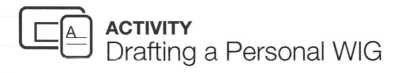

ACTIVITY
Drafting a Personal WIG

Now it is your turn to make an attempt at creating a personal WIG. Do not worry about getting it perfect the first time. This is just a draft.

There are multiple sources you can turn to for identifying a personal WIG.

- *The 7 Habits of Highly Effective People* (See the self-assessment in the Appendix.)

- Your Professional Learning Plan.

- Feedback from a principal or trusted associates.

In choosing a personal WIG, the fundamental question to be asked is:

What is the one thing that, if I were to do it more effectively, would have the greatest positive impact on my effectiveness?

Write your answer to the above question in the space below, then use the worksheet on the following two pages to draft a personal WIG based on what you have chosen. Choose a WIG you would be willing to share with students.

MY PERSONAL WIG

The "one thing" I can do to be more effective is…

Make eating nutritias food

PERSONAL WIG PLANNING WORKSHEET

FOCUS ON THE WILDLY IMPORTANT

What is the "end in mind"?

eating better foods to fuel my body

eat junk food on weekends	—enjoy small treats occasionally	Nov. 1st
Where I am now.	Where I want to be.	By when.

ACT ON THE LEAD MEASURES

What one or two strategies or behavior changes will most help you achieve the WIG?

- drink 1 gal water/day - no soda

- cut out junk food from my normal routine (especially on weekends)

CREATE A CADENCE OF ACCOUNTABILITY

My Accountability Partner(s) is:

When and where we will meet is:

How we will celebrate is:

KEEP A COMPELLING SCOREBOARD

How I will track my lead measures:

- 1 gallon of water drank.

- day went + junk food

How I will track progress toward the "Y" (the lead measure):

- Keep accountability chart

Personal WIG Summary

	PLAN (Mental Creation)	**EXECUTE** (Physical Creation)
Focus on the Wildly Important	• Identify the single most leveraged thing that will impact your effectiveness. • Determine where you are (X). • Establish where you want to be (Y). • Set a *when*. • Clarify *why* the WIG is important.	• Post the WIG in a visible place. • Refer to the WIG and the why often.
Act on the Lead Measures	• Identify critical steps/processes that will lead to the achievement of your WIG. • Select the two or three most leveraged actions that will lead to you achieving your WIG. • Determine the lead measures. • Create a plan for addressing the lead measures.	• Act on the lead measures. • Maintain the "whirlwind." • Say no to unimportant tasks.
Keep a Compelling Scoreboard	• Include both lead measures and lag measures in the scoreboard. • Set goal lines when appropriate. • Meet the five-second rule.	• Post the scoreboard in a visible place. • Update the scoreboard weekly, if not more often.
Create a Cadence of Accountability	• Identify an Accountability Partner. • Set weekly time (short and undivided).	• Meet at a designated time. • Report on commitments. • Update and review the scoreboard. • Make new commitments. • Adjust as needed. (Is the goal still realistic? Is the meeting time working? Do we have the right lead measures? etc.) • Celebrate!

Notes

Notes

Achieving Team (Class) WIGs

- The 4 Disciplines in Teams
- Gallery of Team (Class) WIGs
- Setting a Team (Class) WIG

Achieving Team (Class) WIGs

Just as individuals benefit from utilizing the 4 Disciplines to achieve their highest priorities, teams can also benefit. Teams come in all different sizes and with varying types of goals. Often a person will belong to two or more teams within a school.

This section of the Field Guide explores some of the benefits, challenges, and cautions that come with working in teams to achieve goals. Because the most common teams within a school tend to be a class team or a grade-level team, these teams will receive special emphasis. However, the same principles apply to most any team.

The designed outcomes for this section of the guide are:

- To enable you to become a more effective team member.

- To begin applying the 4 Disciplines in team settings, including with students.

- To enable all school teams (but particularly classrooms) to begin setting and achieving goals.

GRADE-LEVEL TEAM   CAFETERIA TEAM   CLASSROOM

FAMILY

SPECIALTY TEAM   LIGHTHOUSE TEAM   OFFICE TEAM

"As a blind person, I knew I could never get to the summit of Everest alone. And what would get me to the top wasn't necessarily technology; what would get me to the summit were the people that I surrounded myself with."

ERIK WEIHENMAYER

The 4 Disciplines in Teams

Whenever multiple people are brought together and expected to carry out a team WIG, additional attention needs to be given to ensure that all team members are clear about the end in mind.

Keys to pursuing a team WIG include:

INVOLVE PEOPLE.
The overarching principle to consider when striving to achieve a team WIG is: "No involvement, no commitment." People need to feel ownership if they are to put their whole person—body, heart, mind, and spirit—into a goal.

PRODUCE SYNERGY.
Highly effective teams maximize people's strengths and make weaknesses irrelevant. The key is that everyone know her or his role in the goal.

CREATE VISIBILITY.
Goals that are hidden away in file drawers and never spoken of are of little worth. Goals need to be visible and alive daily.

HOLD WIG SESSIONS.
WIG Sessions are opportunities for people to report their contributions, for the team to recalibrate for what will come next, and to measure progress.

CELEBRATE MILESTONES.
Big achievements come from multiple little successes. Celebrate progress at meaningful milestones, not just at the finish line.

Fundamental Rule:
No involvement, no commitment.

The 4 Disciplines in Teams

This video talks about achieving a WIG as a team. Compared to setting personal WIGs, what do you think needs to be done differently…

When setting a WIG as a team?

When students are involved in setting a team WIG?

Discipline 1: Focus on the Wildly Important

 BRAINSTORM A LIST OF WILDLY IMPORTANT GOALS.

It is important that each team member have an opportunity for her or his voice to be heard. Note that:

- Synergistic brainstorming occurs when there is high trust and people do not evaluate or discard others' ideas until all ideas are expressed and fully understood.

- Often the "second-best" ideas are suggested first. The best ideas come after the team discusses the original ideas and uses them to create a 3rd Alternative.

- You need to beware of groupthink.

 TIP: Always remember, what is wildly important to one person may not be wildly important to another. So take the time to Think Win-Win, Seek First to Understand, and Synergize when choosing a WIG that involves multiple people.

 NARROW THE LIST TO ONE TEAM WIG.

A team should have no more than one or two team WIGs. In narrowing your team's choices, ask, "What is the one change that will have the greatest impact on the team's effectiveness?" Note that:

- School administrators may veto a specific WIG but should not dictate a WIG.

- Because a person's idea for a WIG was not selected does not mean it cannot be pursued at a later time or is a less important goal.

- Eighty percent of the team's energy will continue to be directed at maintaining the whirlwind. Many other goals are still important and should not be ignored.

WRITE THE TEAM WIG IN A "FROM X TO Y BY WHEN" FORMAT.

Goals become useful when written and stated in specific, realistic terms that include:

X = Where is the team now? The "Starting Line."

Y = Where does the team want to be? The "Finish Line."

WHEN = Over what period of time will the achievement of the WIG be spread? "The Deadline."

EXAMPLE: *We will go from averaging 25 discipline referrals per month as a grade-level team to averaging 10 discipline referrals per month by the end of the term.*

 POST THE WIG IN A VISIBLE LOCATION.

Place the WIG in a visible location where all team members can see it often and refer to it in team WIG Sessions. Note that:

- Team WIGs that are kept in a drawer or on the leader's desk will not be transferred into results.

- Ensure that all team members are clear as to why the WIG is important. Remind them often of that *why*.

> "Goals cannot sound bold but vague. Targets cannot be so blurry they can't be hit. Your direction has to be so vivid that if you randomly woke one of your employees in the middle of the night and asked him, "Where are we going?" he could still answer in a half-asleep stupor."
>
> JACK WELCH

Discipline 2: Act on the Lead Measures

 IDENTIFY A LIST OF STRATEGIES FOR ACHIEVING THE TEAM WIG.

Identify specific behaviors that need to be changed or action steps that will "lead" to the team WIG being achieved.

- Be realistic. You can always increase or decrease the number or scope of your action steps later.

- If this is a project-based WIG, you may want to create a timeline, Flow-chart, or Gantt Chart to identify action steps.

 SELECT THE ONE OR TWO STRATEGIES WITH THE HIGHEST LEVERAGE.

Identify the one or two strategies (strategic bets) generated from the above list that, if implemented well, will have the greatest impact on the team's ability and likelihood of achieving the WIG. Things to consider include:

- If the team has data on its effectiveness or outcomes, what are the greatest gaps?

- What best practices have other teams implemented to achieve the same type of WIG?

- What barriers may interfere?

- Who on the team will complete each strategy and action step?

 TIP: Remember, the highest-leveraged action steps should be:
Predictive: "I bet if we do this action step, it will lead to the team WIG being achieved." *Influenceable:* Within the team's Circle of Influence and capacity.

③ TURN THE HIGHEST-LEVERAGED STRATEGIES INTO LEAD MEASURES.

Many teams make the mistake of only measuring the outcomes they desire to achieve (their Y). Successful goal-achieving teams also track progress on their lead measures. For example, if your grade-level team goal is to reduce discipline referrals to 10 per month, then your lead measures might be:

Lead Measure 1

Spend one-on-one time with each student once each week to build a relationship.

Lead Measure 2

Give each student a leadership role.

Outcome (Y)

Reduce discipline referrals to an average of 10 per month.

④ ACT ON THE TEAM'S LEAD MEASURES.

Being able to divide and conquer is one advantage of pursuing a team WIG. Other advantages include:

- Individuals with different strengths can take on action steps unique to their skillset, while others can take on action steps unique to their skillset. Quality improves.

- Working in teams reduces boredom. People can cheer others on and offer advice.

- Work can be completed in a smaller time span.

- Synergy!

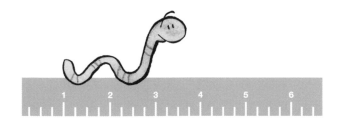

Discipline 3: Keep a Compelling Scoreboard

 CREATE A SCOREBOARD.

Scoreboards are even more important in team situations. People not only deserve but need to know where they are and how far they need to go to achieve their goal. A typical team scoreboard displays:

1. How the team is progressing in completing its lead measures.

2. How the team is progressing toward the overall WIG (the Y).

2 **GIVE IT THE "COMPELLING" TEST.**

Team scoreboards that are complicated or display too much data can be more demotivating than compelling. Characteristics of a compelling scoreboard include:

1. The scoreboard is engaging to the eye.

2. In five seconds or less, a person can tell if the team is "winning" or "losing" in its quest to achieve its WIG.

3. It shows a goal line. (See "Beat the Goat" on the next page.)

4. It is designed to emphasize progress. Success breeds success.

5. An individual can discern how his or her efforts contribute to team outcomes by looking at the team scoreboard.

"Conventional thinking is that scoreboards are for leaders. The 4 Disciplines way of thinking is that scoreboards are for the whole team."

THE 4 DISCIPLINES

③ PLACE THE SCOREBOARD IN A VISIBLE LOCATION.

Place the scoreboard where team members can see it often and refer to in meetings. It may need to be in more than one location or available digitally for people not local. Less important is how it is made visible than that it is made visible and updateable on a consistent basis. No athlete wants to wait until the end of the game to learn the final score, and so it is with other types of teams.

BEAT THE GOAT
A way to make scoreboards compelling and fun is to make a game of it—to flip the "Game on!" switch. One way to do this is to "beat the goat." The goat represents the "goal line" or where the team should be if it is progressing at the desired rate. If a team is "beating the goat," that means they are ahead of where they should be. At each measurement period, the team can see if they are "beating the goat," and celebrate milestones.

EXAMPLE: *Say a team has a WIG to have every student hold a meaningful school-level leadership role by the end of the year. On average, this means that 25 percent of students will have filled a role by the end of the first quarter, 50 percent by the end of the second quarter, and a 100 percent at the end of the year. The path is represented by the goat. The "Game on!" switch happens as team members work to "beat the goat" and complete the goal sooner than expected.*

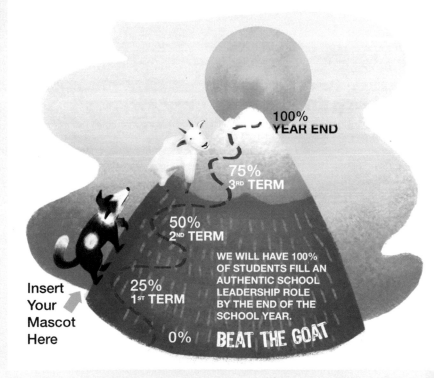

100%
YEAR END

75%
3ʳᵈ TERM

50%
2ᴺᴰ TERM

WE WILL HAVE 100% OF STUDENTS FILL AN AUTHENTIC SCHOOL LEADERSHIP ROLE BY THE END OF THE SCHOOL YEAR.

Insert Your Mascot Here

25%
1ˢᵗ TERM

0% BEAT THE GOAT

Discipline 4: Create a Cadence of Accountability

 HOLD WEEKLY WIG SESSIONS AT A CONSISTENT TIME.

If a team is small, all members of the team are encouraged to participate in developing a cadence of accountability. If a team is large—more than 15 people—a smaller subteam may be selected to represent the voice of the whole.

Meet on a consistent basis, at least once a week. This is called a WIG Session. A best practice is for the team to meet on the same day of the week and at the same time, with rare exception. The WIG Session helps keep WIGs from getting lost and forgotten in the whirlwind.

 FOLLOW A CONSISTENT, FOCUSED AGENDA.

Keep WIG Sessions short and focused. While the content may vary, the agenda remains consistent.

- Account: Report on commitments. "Did we do what we committed to each other we would do?"

- Review and update the scoreboard: Learn from successes and failures.

- Plan: Make new commitments. Each new commitment should meet two standards: First, the commitment must represent a specific deliverable; and second, the commitment must influence the lead measures.

 TIP: The whirlwind is never allowed into a WIG Session, no matter how urgent an issue may seem. Keeping your WIG Sessions to 20 to 30 minutes is a standard to strive for. To prepare for the session, every team member thinks about the same question: "What are the one or two most important things I can do this week to impact the lead measures?

ADJUST AS NECESSARY.

WIGs and lead measures may need to be adjusted on occasion. WIGs should be set high enough to be motivational and low enough to be attainable. Make sure your measuring stick is appropriate for the team as a whole.

 TIP: If people are running into obstacles in keeping their commitments, team members can commit to clear the path for each other or reassign the task.

CELEBRATE MILESTONES, NOT JUST THE FINISH LINE.

Celebrate even small successes as a team. Reinforce commitment to the WIG by congratulating both the team and individual members on successfully keeping commitments and moving the measures.

"We set up a nightly tent meeting because it was a very effective way to get a lot of communication across."

P. V. SCATURRO, EVEREST CLIMBING–TEAM LEADER

"The tent meetings seemed incredibly important. The ability to have an open forum to communicate, to talk about things, it gets you thinking."

ERIC, CLIMBING–TEAM MEMBER

Gallery of Team (Class) WIGs

Team WIGs can be created to address most any need a team may have. The following video and gallery of photos emphasize grade-level and team WIGs. But WIGs can be designed to meet any type of team challenge. Samples include:

LIBRARY: Improving the number of books returned on time, increasing the number of student leaders helping in library.

OFFICE/ADMINISTRATION: Increasing staff satisfaction, improving parent relationships, raising funds, increasing attendance, cutting costs.

PLAYGROUND: Reducing the incidences of bullying, reducing the number of injuries, increasing fitness participation.

CAFETERIA: Reducing food waste, increasing recycling, improving nutrition.

CUSTODIAL: Improving hallway cleanliness, reducing chair setup times.

GRADE-LEVEL: Raising reading fluency, reduced discipline referrals.

CLASS: Academics, attendance, in-class behavior, cleanliness, straight lines.

VIDEO
Team WIGs

Watch the video and gather ideas for creating team WIGs. Then work as a team to complete the following activity:

PART 1: Select one of the sample challenges from the previous page and write it in a "From X to Y by When" format.

PART 2: What are some key action steps that need to be taken in order to achieve the "From X to Y by When" goal? Which two are the highest-leveraged (the ones you will use as lead measures)?

PART 3: How might you scoreboard (1) the lead measures, and (2) the overall outcome (lag measure, or Y) you are trying to achieve?

PART 4: What will you do to "Create a Cadence of Accountability"?

"When team members regard each other with mutual respect, differences are utilized and are considered strengths rather than weaknesses. The role of the leader is to foster mutual respect and build a complementary team where each person's strength is made productive and each person's weakness irrelevant."

STEPHEN R. COVEY

Grade-Level Team WIGs.

Explore the team WIGs and the variety of scoreboards on the following pages to consider various types of WIGs a team you belong to might pursue. Which aspects do you like or dislike about the various approaches? Team WIGs need to be written and designed in a way that matches the nature of the team, so there is no "one and only" way.

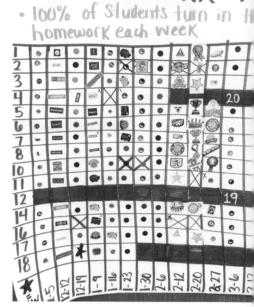

OUR HOMEWORK GO
- 100% of students turn in th homework each week

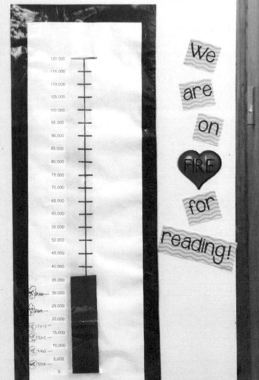

As a grade level, our W.I.G. is to read 120,000 minutes by the end of 2nd grade.

We are on ❤️ FIRE for reading!

By February 6th, 80% of 5th grad students will be secure in finding the main idea and at lea two supporting details and identify the text structure of a non-fictio passage.

Baseline: 4%

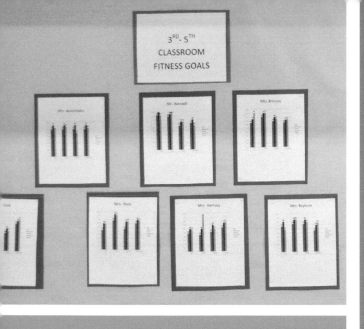

3RD - 5TH
CLASSROOM
FITNESS GOALS

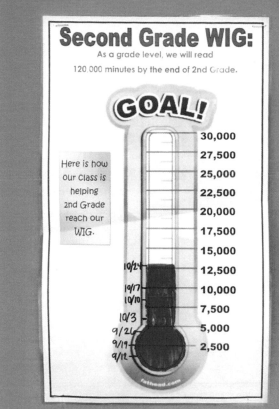

Second Grade WIG:

As a grade level, we will read
120,000 minutes by the end of 2nd Grade.

GOAL!

Here is how our Class is helping 2nd Grade reach our WIG.

Date	Minutes
	30,000
	27,500
	25,000
	22,500
	20,000
	17,500
	15,000
10/24	12,500
10/17	10,000
10/10	7,500
10/3	5,000
9/26	
9/19	2,500
9/12	

fathead.com

100% of

Hooray!!!
We met this goal!

1st Graders will identify a leader and describe the qualities of a good leader.

© Franklin Covey Co.

65

Reading	100% of students will read 120 WCPM or increase by 20% with 98% accuracy on Fluency practice tests, progress monitoring through DIBELS
Math	100% of all students will be able to identify fractions, mixed numbers, and decimals with 90% accuracy on grade level common assessment.
Writing	100% of students will be able to produce clear coherent writing and receive a cumulative score of 16 or higher using a combination of Utah Compose and sage writing points

LOOK AT HOW MANY BOOKS 5TH GRADE HAS READ!

All first graders will solve a minimum of 17 addition problems correctly in two minutes by the end of this school year.

By January 30, 80% of all 3rd grade students will consistently and accurately complete 95-100 subtraction facts in 5 minutes.

ng Number Corner

5th Grade Goals

Reading 1st Quarter Average:	Reading 2nd Quarter Average:	Reading 3rd Quarter Average:	Math 1st Quarter Average:	Math 2nd Quarter Average:	Math 3rd Quarter Average:
701	747	803	738	762	777

Goal by May   +30=833

Goal by May   +30=807

Gallery of Class WIGs

Study the following examples of team WIGs. Think about what types of WIGs your class might pursue that would engage students.

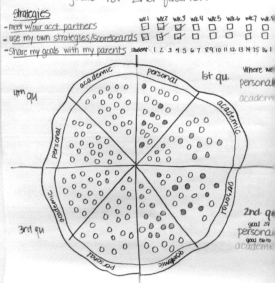

We will go from 29% to 40% of our students reaching their personal goals and 56% to 67% of our students reaching their academic goals for 2nd quarter.

SYNERGIZE
to reach our classroom Home Reading goal!

By Dec. 1st our goal is 10,000 minutes!

Each snowflake equals 100 minutes!

Classroom Goal

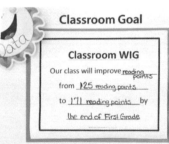

Classroom WIG

Our class will improve reading points from 125 reading points to 171 reading points by the end of First Grade

Goal Tracking

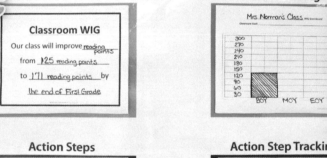

Mrs. Norman's Class

300
270
240
210
180
150
120
90
60
30

BOY   MOY   EOY

Action Steps

Classroom Action Steps

1. Read to Self
2. Word Work
3. Reading Groups

Action Step Tracking

Mrs. Norman's Class

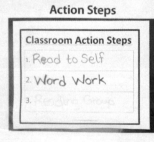

Homework Leader?
Miss Meckel's Class

GOAL 90%

92 % out of 100% have completed our homework.

Homework Leader?
Mr. McClain's Class

GOAL 100%

95 % out of 100% have completed our homework.

LEADERS Begin with the End in Mind

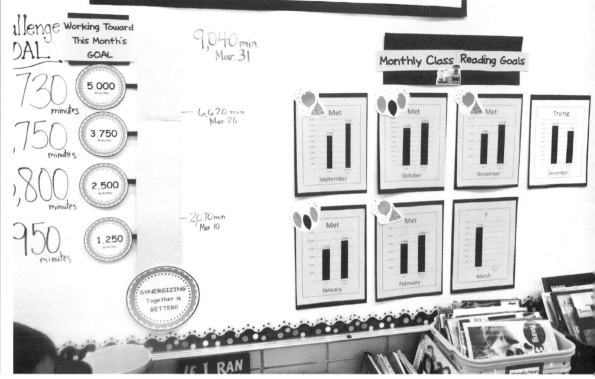

...llenge
...DAL.

Working Toward This Month's GOAL

730 minutes — 5,000 minutes

...750 minutes — 3,750 minutes

...800 minutes — 2,500 minutes

...950 minutes — 1,250 minutes

9,040 min. Mar. 31

6,620 min Mar. 26

2,070 min Mar 10

SYNERGIZING Together is BETTER!!

Monthly Class Reading Goals

| September | October | November | December |
| Met | Met | Met | Trying |

| January | February | March |
| Met | Met | ? |

Our class will score 6 **All** **Time** **Best** out of our 9 unit assessments in Science + SS this 9 wks.

Strategies — 1 per week each

- partner study sessions ●●●●●○○○○ 1 2 3 4 5 6 7 8 9
- file folder games ●●●●○○○○○ 1 2 3 4 5 6 7 8 9
- subject journaling with leadership tools ●●●●●○○○○ 1 2 3 4 5 6 7 8 9

Science and SS Unit Test

(bar chart: WK1, WK2, WK3, WK4, WK5, WK6, WK7, WK8, WK9 — bars marked ATB, ATB2, ATB3)

franklincovey

Our Goal {6} ATB

Will we do it?

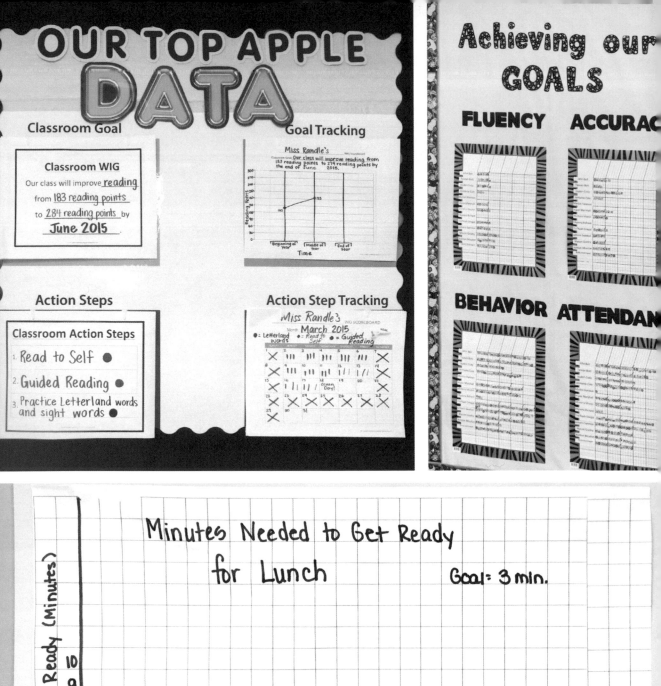

OUR TOP APPLE DATA

Classroom Goal

Classroom WIG

Our class will improve _reading_ from _183 reading points_ to _284 reading points_ by **June 2015**.

Goal Tracking

Miss Randle's

Classroom Goal: Our class will improve reading from 183 reading points to 279 reading points by the end of June 2015.

Action Steps

Classroom Action Steps

1. Read to Self ●
2. Guided Reading ●
3. Practice Letterland words and sight words ●

Action Step Tracking

Miss Randle's
March 2015 WIG SCOREBOARD

● = Letterland Words ● = Read to Self ● = Guided Reading

Achieving our GOALS

FLUENCY   **ACCURACY**

BEHAVIOR   **ATTENDANCE**

Minutes Needed to Get Ready for Lunch

Goal = 3 min.

Time it Took to Get Ready (Minutes) — 10, 9, 8, 7, 6, 5, 4, 3, 2, 1

Date: 9/18, 9/19, 9/22, 9/23, 9/24, 9/25, 9/26, 9/29, 9/30, 9/1, 10/2, 10/3, 10/6, 10/7, 10/8, 10/9, 10/10, 10/13, 10/14, 10/16, 10/17, 10/20, 10/21, 10/22, 10/23, 10/24, 10/27

70

of Mrs. Madden's 5th grade dents will consistently and accurately complete 100 plication facts in four minutes y September 29, 2014.

8% of students are secure

Mission Accomplished!
Students put first things first and worked hard to meet their goal with 91% of students becoming secure with their multiplication facts! Way to go!

We will increase our independent writing time from 7 to 20 minutes.

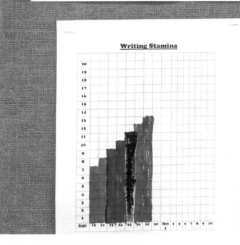

Writing Stamina

oth's Responsible Rock Stars
February   Reading Goal

705

14,957

8

52

76

3046

Our goal is to read 14,705 minutes in February at home.

Our Totals

Week 1	3046
Week 2	4182
Week 3	4088
Week 4	3641
Total	14,15

We met our February goal!

R₃

© Franklin Covey Co.

Literacy Goal: We will have a grade level average of 80% in DIBELS testing at the end of the year.

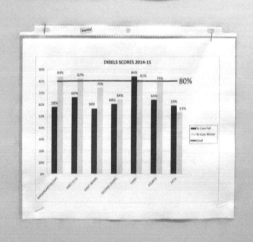

DIBELS SCORES 2014-15

80%

Setting a Team (Class) WIG

Having seen what other teams have done with setting team WIGs, begin exploring WIGs you would like to target as a team. Consider some of the samples below. How would you turn them into WIGs?

NON-CLASS EXAMPLES

- The lunchroom is a noisy, messy place. It doesn't look or feel like "leadership."

- Too many students are lonely on the playground.

- The office staff wants to increase its involvement in *The Leader in Me*.

- We need more parent volunteers to read with Grade 1 students.

- The custodial team wants to increase the number of student volunteers to set up and take down for assemblies.

- Our grade-level team needs to share ideas more.

CLASS EXAMPLES

- Our classroom walls are uninspiring.

- The same five students always fill the main leadership roles in our class.

- We can't seem to find time for class meetings.

- It would really help to have non-instructional staff read to students.

- We need to raise our math scores.

- We have serious problems with attendance and tardies.

- There are a lot of students talking during quiet reading time.

- It takes the teacher 20 minutes each night to shut down the room (e.g., turn off computers, straighten chairs, close blinds, shut off lights).

ACTIVITY
Creating a Team WIG

It is now your turn to create a team WIG. When choosing a team WIG, the fundamental question is:

What is the one thing that, if we were to do it more effectively as a team, would have the greatest positive impact on the team's effectiveness?

There are multiple sources you can turn to for identifying a team WIG, including:

- Look at the School Improvement Plan and choose a goal that will contribute to the school's goal.

- Examine challenges your team is currently having regarding leadership, culture, or academics. Choose one of those challenges and make a WIG around it. (See samples on the previous page.)

- Pick a simple goal students will want to pursue as a way of learning the 4 Disciplines.

In a team you belong to, use one of the above sources to select one thing to work on as a team and write it in the space below. Then use the worksheet on the following two pages to draft a team WIG plan based on that choice.

The "one thing" the team can do to be more effective is...

TEAM WIG PLANNING WORKSHEET

FOCUS ON THE WILDLY IMPORTANT

What is the "end in mind"?

Where we are now.	Where we want to be.	By when.

ACT ON THE LEAD MEASURES

What one or two strategies will best help us achieve the WIG?

CREATE A CADENCE OF ACCOUNTABILITY

Our accountability team will be:

When and where we will meet is:

How we will celebrate is:

KEEP A COMPELLING SCOREBOARD

How we will track our lead measures:

How we will track progress toward our "Y" (end in mind):

ACHIEVING TEAM (CLASS) WIGS

Team (Class) WIG Summary

	PLAN (Mental Creation)	**EXECUTE** (Physical Creation)
Focus on the Wildly Important	• Involve team members in identifying the single most leveraged task that will impact your team's (class's) effectiveness. • Determine where the team is (X). • Establish where the team wants to be (Y). • Set a *when*. • Clarify *why* the WIG is important.	• Post the WIG in a visible place where team members will see it on a regular basis. • Refer to the WIG and the why often.
Act on the Lead Measures	• Identify critical steps/processes that will lead to the achievement of the team WIG. • Select the two or three most-leveraged strategies or actions that will lead to you achieving the WIG. • Determine lead measures. • Create a plan for addressing the lead measures. • Clearly identify who on the team will complete which parts of the lead measures.	• Act on the lead measures. • Maintain the "whirlwind." • Say no to unimportant tasks.
Keep a Compelling Scoreboard	• Include both lead measures and lag measures in the scoreboard. • Set goal lines when appropriate. • Meet the five-second rule.	• Post the scoreboard in a visible place. • Update the scoreboard weekly, if not more often.
Create a Cadence of Accountability	• Identify the accountability team. • Set weekly time (short and undivided) for WIG Sessions.	• Meet at a designated time. • Report on commitments. • Update and review the scoreboard. • Make new commitments. • Adjust as needed. (Is the goal still realistic? Is the meeting time working? Do we have the right lead measures? etc.) • Celebrate!

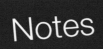

Notes

ACHIEVING TEAM (CLASS) WIGS

Achieving
Student WIGs

- The 4 Disciplines With Students
- Gallery of Student WIGs
- Setting a Student WIG
- Leadership Notebooks
- Student-Led Conferences

Achieving Student WIGs

Students truly enjoy pursuing meaningful goals. They see it as a game. In contrast, when goals are unrealistic or used as "sticks" to put students on guilt trips, goals have a demotivating effect. Therefore, it is important that goal setting be handled well when working with students.

This section of the Field Guide looks at how to lead students toward learning how to set and achieve goals on their own. Even though students must own the goal themselves for it to be truly effective, having an insightful, caring adult working with them—especially younger students—goes a long way toward making a student's goal practical, achievable, and motivating.

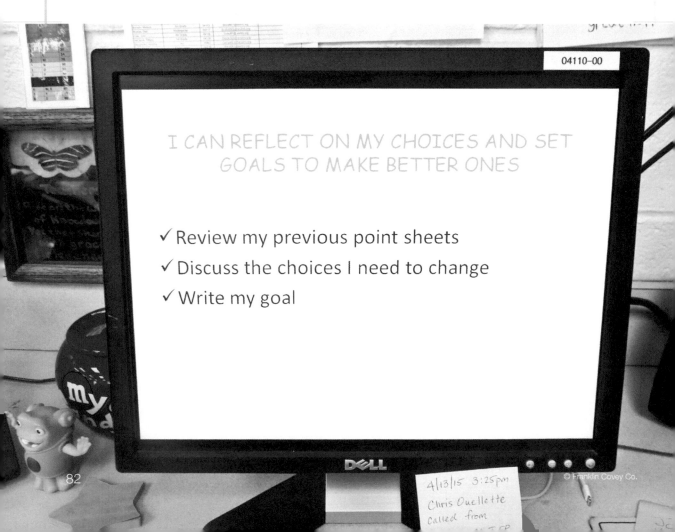

I CAN REFLECT ON MY CHOICES AND SET GOALS TO MAKE BETTER ONES

✓ Review my previous point sheets
✓ Discuss the choices I need to change
✓ Write my goal

The designed outcomes for this section of the guide are:

- To empower students to help themselves achieve their goals.
- To enable you to be more effective in helping students achieve goals.
- To provide two tools for students to take more ownership for their progress.

> "I realized at that moment that he's a guy I want to support his dream. And I, I said to him, 'I don't know if I'm strong enough to get to the top, Erik, but I know I'm strong enough to help you get there.'"
>
> ERIK'S CLIMBING–TEAM PARTNER

The 4 Disciplines **With Students**

At first glance, some of the concepts connected with the 4 Disciplines may appear larger than what young students can grasp developmentally. However, when students see adults modeling the 4 Disciplines and when the language is presented in simple and fun ways, students grasp the concepts quickly.

1. **FOCUS ON THE WILDLY IMPORTANT** (Choose Your WIG)

2. **ACT ON THE LEAD MEASURES** (Take the Key Steps)

3. **KEEP A COMPELLING SCOREBOARD** (Keep Score)

4. **CREATE A CADENCE OF ACCOUNTABILITY** (Huddle Up)

The 4 Disciplines Mountain

Discipline 1:
FOCUS ON THE WILDLY IMPORTANT
Choose Your WIG

Discipline 4:
CREATE A CADENCE OF ACCOUNTABILITY
Huddle Up

Discipline 3:
KEEP A COMPELLING SCOREBOARD
Keep Score

Discipline 2:
ACT ON THE LEAD MEASURES
Take the Key Steps

VIDEO
Students WIGs

This video offers examples of how educators use the 4 Disciplines to set goals with students.

What insights do the educators provide regarding to how to teach students goal setting?

What benefits do students experience from achieving goals?

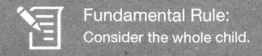

Fundamental Rule:
Consider the whole child.

Discipline 1: Focus on the Wildly Important

 BRAINSTORM A LIST OF WILDLY IMPORTANT GOALS WITH STUDENTS.

Help students feel the worth of working on something important and know what "important" means. Begin by:

- In a group setting (perhaps as an entire class), listen to what students feel is of greatest worth that they can work on personally. Simply ask, for example: "What is the one thing that, if you were to do it better, would make you a better student?" Or leader in the classroom? Or whatever fits the situation.

- If needed, expand students' thinking by sharing ideas and important goals you think they can achieve or that other students have achieved.

 TIP: Students want to feel of worth. Working on something important helps them feel that worth. Consider the whole child.

 NARROW THE LIST TO ONE STUDENT WIG.

Students generally have more good ideas for WIGs than they can ever pursue. Help them:

- See the value of pursuing one WIG at a time.

- Identify one WIG that is achievable in the near future. They can become superheroes in later years, but for now, focus on something they can do within a month or so.

- Have students tell or write why the goal is important to them.

 TIP: It is highly recommended that students choose a WIG that will make an impact at school, such as working on getting better at one of the 7 Habits or other ways to be a leader.

WRITE THE WIG IN A "FROM X TO Y BY WHEN" FORMAT.

Help students understand that goals are most useful when written in specific, realistic terms that include:

X = Where are they now? Their "Starting Line."

Y = Where do they want to be? Their "Finish Line."

WHEN = Over what period of time will the achievement of the WIG be spread? Their "Deadline."

 TIP: Early on, this should be made as fun and simple as possible. Students who have successes with goal setting are more likely to continue the process.

 HAVE STUDENTS PUT THEIR WIG IN A VISIBLE LOCATION.

This can include one or more options, such as:

- In their Leadership Notebook (to be described later).

- Written on a small card and taped to a corner of their desk.

Discipline 2: Act on the Lead Measures

 IDENTIFY A LIST OF STRATEGIES FOR ACHIEVING THE STUDENT WIG.

Work with the student to identify specific strategies or behaviors to be changed that will "lead" to the goal being achieved. With increases in age and maturity, each student will be able to identify action steps on his or her own. Guide toward action steps that are within the student's Circle of Influence and will have a direct impact on the child achieving his or her WIG. Consider the whole child—body, heart, mind, and spirit.

If the WIG is an academic WIG, the student will likely need help in identifying what the action steps—or strategies—will be. Nevertheless, the more the child is involved in planning, the more he or she will be engaged in the process.

 SELECT THE ONE OR TWO STRATEGIES WITH THE HIGHEST LEVERAGE.

Identify the one or two strategies from the list that have the greatest potential to impact the student's chances of achieving the WIG.

TIP: Particularly if this is the student's first WIG, make the action steps doable and as enjoyable as possible. The intent is that he or she learn the process and have success with it. As the student matures, he or she will be able to select more challenging action items.

❸ TURN THE HIGHEST-LEVERAGE STRATEGIES INTO LEAD MEASURES.

Students might not fully understand the concept of lead measures initially, but they can be taught the concept over time. At a minimum, they should be able to clearly understand when a strategy is completed so they can check it off when they have completed it.

Lead Measure 1

Read 20 minutes every day.

WIG ("From X to Y by When")

Improve one reading grade by the end of the quarter.

Lead Measure 2

Attend school each day I'm not sick.

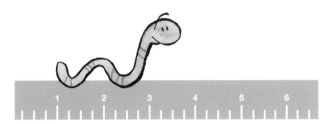

❹ TAKE DIRECT ACTION ON THE LEAD MEASURES.

Initially, the strategies may be best completed in class, or at least somewhere at school. In other words, allow students time in class to act on their lead measures rather than expecting them to do it on their own time and at home.

ACHIEVING STUDENT WIGS

Discipline 3: Keep a Compelling Scoreboard

 CREATE A STUDENT-FRIENDLY SCOREBOARD.

Students behave differently when they keep score. Keeping score is commonly done by teachers in grade books. But when pursuing WIGs, some of that responsibility is passed to students to track for themselves.

A student-friendly scoreboard displays:

1. Progress toward the desired outcome; shows where students "are" in their progress relative to the actual goal (Y).

   EXAMPLE: *Display where the student is in regard to achieving grade level at reading.*

2. Progress on the lead measures. Show on the scoreboard if students completed their strategies. Students love to bubble in progress on a chart.

   EXAMPLE: *Each day check off on a monthly calendar if the student read for 20 minutes.*

3. A powerful motivator is to create a "goal" line for the students to exceed. It creates a "Game on!" mindset. A popular motivator is for students to try to "beat the goat."

   EXAMPLE: *A reading chart that shows a goat climbing at a rate of 20 minutes a day. The student's actual reading rate is measured separately, showing the score relative to the goat's rate. The goal is to show the student beating the goat.*

"Beat the goat."

GIVE THE SCOREBOARD THE "COMPELLING" TEST.

Scoreboards that are complicated or show too much data can be more confusing and discouraging than compelling. Characteristics of a compelling scoreboard include:

1. It contains both desired outcomes (Y) and lead measures.

2. In five seconds or less, a student can tell if he or she is "winning" in the progress to meet or beat the goal.

3. It shows progress. Students like to see progress.

4. It's fun and engaging.

 TIP: Perhaps the most engaging factor in a compelling scoreboard is if it shows progress. Students like to see that they are progressing on a consistent basis. Flat lines are not motivating.

 PLACE THE SCOREBOARD IN A VISIBLE LOCATION AND UPDATE OFTEN.

When students see positive results happening from their efforts, they become more engaged. So their scoreboard should be kept in a highly visible place where they can see it frequently.

 TIP: Leadership Notebooks (to be discussed shortly) are the prime location for students to display their scoreboards.

Discipline 4: Create a Cadence of Accountability

 IDENTIFY AN ACCOUNTABILITY PARTNER FOR EACH STUDENT.

When students have a partner to account to—someone they trust—they are more likely to achieve a WIG. Often they fondly refer to their partner as their "accountabili-buddy." It should be a person they trust, who's available on a steady basis, and who can give good feedback. Consider using:

- Teachers.
- Peers.
- Parents.
- Older mentor students.

 TIP: A key role of an Accountability Partner is to help students see their worth. This happens as they continuously keep in mind the definition of leadership below:

The key role of an Accountability Partner for students is to be a leader—to cheer them on, compliment them, give feedback on strategies, and help them be realistic. When students have Accountability Partners they trust and relate to, they do their best to achieve their goal.

"Leadership is communicating people's worth and potential so clearly that they are inspired to see it in themselves."

STEPHEN R. COVEY

② MEET AT A CONSISTENT TIME.

Most students will need help in setting up a regular meeting time with their Accountability Partner. Typically, this will happen during class or another appropriate time. For example, if the student is working on a reading WIG, it will likely occur during reading time. Accountability sessions include:

1. Report on previous commitments. ("How is it going?")

2. Review and update the scoreboard. ("Let's look at your scoreboard.")

3. Make new commitments. ("Next week I am going to read five minutes more each day.")

③ ADJUST AS NECESSARY.

Occasionally, the original WIG or lead measures may need to be adjusted. WIGs should be challenging enough to be motivational; achievable enough to be attainable. Make sure each student's measuring stick is the appropriate length for her or his needs. Help them learn from successes and failures.

④ CELEBRATE MILESTONES, NOT JUST THE FINISH LINE.

Intrinsic rewards have more meaning and last longer than extrinsic rewards. Though extrinsic rewards can be very motivating to students, external rewards must be attached to intrinsic rewards to have full and lasting value.

Gallery of Student WIGs

Study the following examples of student WIGs. Some deal with nonacademic goals; others focus on academic goals. Look for:

How are the goals adapted for various age levels?

Which scoreboards do you think are most motivating for students?

What would you do to improve the goals?

1st Trimester Reflection
November, 2014

1st grade ROCKS

Something I'm PROUD of...
I am PROUD of all of my reading I do at Home.

My favorite part of the day is...
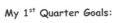
because I can
Art Pat
paint

A goal I'm working on is:
I want to read at a level I.

A step that will help me achieve my goal is:
I am going to read I extra book everyday.

Tanri   1-13-15

Academic Goal

Goal SS		
not getting the resolbhon X	getting the resolshon Y	march 12th 2015
to	**by**	
Where I am now	Where I want to be	Date

Steps to reach my goal
1. read books at my leveal and do SS
2. Compar ss with a friend

My Assessment
SS robric

My 1st Quarter Goals:
10-12-12

My personal goal is...

My goal is to de my bk with ot chawie wrds.

My academic goal is...

y goal is to n bo site urs.

© Franklin Covey Co.

Writing Goals

Use spaces between words
I_like_to_eat_pizza.

Capital Letters
i → I

Punctuation to end my sentences
That was a huge star!

Spelling
wen ⟶ When
lik ⟶ like

Sparkle Words The dog ran ~~fast~~ as fast as a jet.

Add more detail Who? How? When? What? Where? Why?

95

_____ Academic WIG

(NAME)   **WILDY IMPORTANT GOAL**

CHOOSE ONE:

Aa

I will… Learn all my letter sounds by the end of December. I will measure with a tracking chart by coloring in the letters I know as I learn the sounds.

**99..
100**

I will… Count to 100 by April. I will measure this by coloring in a "hundred numbers" tracking chart.

I will… Read all my popcorn words by May. I will measure this by coloring words I can read on a chart to keep track.

Hannah Ross

I will… Write my first and last name by May. I will measure this by tracking when I practice on a calendar.

I will… Turn my homework in on time each day and track it on my homework chart.

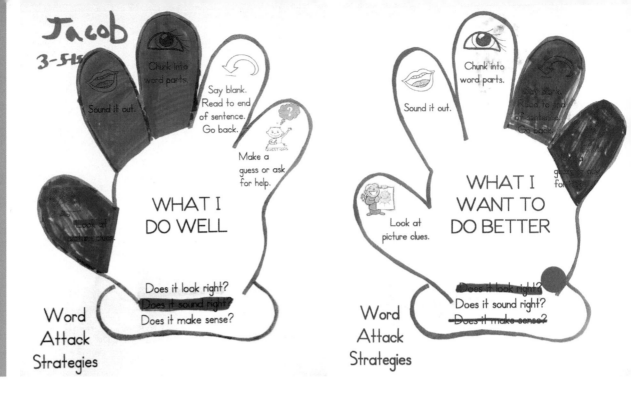

Jacob
3-5-15

WHAT I DO WELL — Word Attack Strategies

- Sound it out.
- Chunk into word parts.
- Say blank. Read to end of sentence. Go back.
- Make a guess or ask for help.
- Look at picture clues.
- Does it look right?
- Does it sound right?
- Does it make sense?

WHAT I WANT TO DO BETTER — Word Attack Strategies

- Sound it out.
- Chunk into word parts.
- Say blank. Read to end of sentence. Go back.
- guess or ask for help
- Look at picture clues.
- Does it look right?
- Does it sound right?
- Does it make sense?

My Academic Goal

re: 1-27-15

goal is

— I will be able to say 50 beginning sounds (FSF) of words in one minute
able to read on a level C by the end of the 3rd nine weeks.

s is important because ___
will be a bettr reder.

o will help me? _____

picture of how I will reach my goal

Unit 3

Spelling/ Vocabulary Goal: I will be proactive and study my spelling and vocabulary words each night.

Spelling

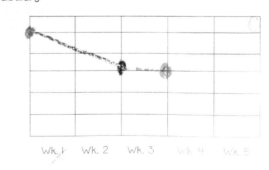

	Week 1	Week 2	Week 3	Week 4	Week 5
100					
90					
80					
70					
60					
50					
40					
30					
20					
10					
Unit 3					

Vocabulary

6 5 4 3 2 1 0

Wk. 1   Wk. 2   Wk. 3   Wk. 4   Wk. 5

I am Responsible for ME

October

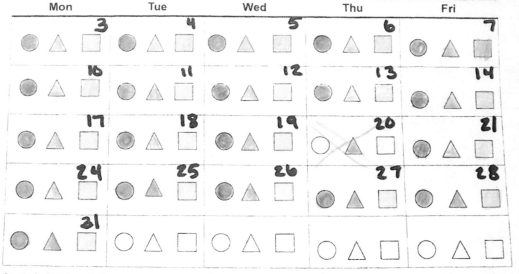

I am "Proactive" I bring my Assignent Book to school.

I make sure I have my communicator folder.

Mon	Tue	Wed	Thu	Fri
3 ● △ □	4 ● △ □	5 ● △ □	6 ● △ □	7 ● △ ■
10 ● △ □	11 ● △ □	12 ● △ □	13 ● △ □	14 ● △ □
17 ● △ □	18 ● △ □	19 ● △ □	20 ○ △ □	21 ● △ □
24 ● △ □	25 ● △ □	26 ● △ □	27 ● △ □	28 ● △ □
31 ● △ □	○ △ □	○ △ □	○ △ □	○ △ □

● Color the circle <u>BLUE</u> each day that you brought your "<u>COMMUNICATOR FOLDER</u>" to school.

△ Color the triangle <u>GREEN</u> for each day you brought in your "<u>WORD STUDY</u>".

□ Color the square <u>YELLOW</u> for each day that you brought your "<u>ASSIGNMENT BOOK</u>" back to school.

Be Proactive

- sprinkles - 11
- whip - 12
  cream

98

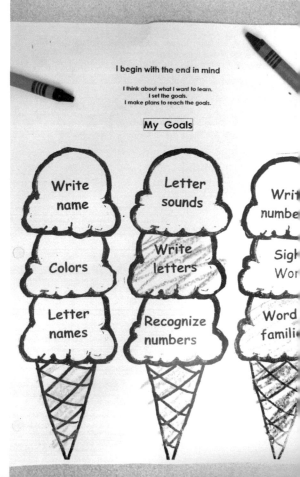

I begin with the end in mind

I think about what I want to learn.
I set the goals.
I make plans to reach the goals.

My Goals

Write name / Colors / Letter names

Letter sounds / Write letters / Recognize numbers

Writ number / Sigh Wor / Word famili

Ethan

Personal Goal

Goal	Name all 36 species of wildcat		
now almost all species of hous cats	Name all 36 species of wild cats	Be spring B. re	
	to	by	
Where I am now	Where I want to be	Date	

Steps to reach my goal

ad 29 miunutes of cut Bats
rootveiw tecnoligy to reuch
o to the libreyry
eekily test (no Books)

Assessment

me all 36 specis of wild cats

What can we do to make our reading goal?

- I can use a timer to help me keep track of my reading minutes
- I will set an alarm
- I will put first things first and read right away when I get home from school
- Read when I have free time- sharpen the saw
- Read before playing electronics

Josiah

Academic Goal: High Frequency Words

a	all	am	and	are	at	be	because
big	boy	but	by	can	come	did	do
down	eat	find	for	from	get	girl	go
good	had	has	have	he	help	here	him
I	in	into	is	it	jump	like	little
look	love	make	me	my	no	not	now
of	on	out	our	play	ran	run	said
saw	say	she	so	some	that	the	then
there	they	this	to	too	up	very	want
was	we	went	what	when	where	who	why
will	with	yes	you				

My Reading Level Growth

	August Beginning	October 1st Q	December 2nd Q	March 3rd Q	May 4th Q
U					
T					
S					
R					
Q					
P					
O					
N					
M					
L					
K					
J					
I					
H					
G					
F					
E					
D					
C					

M   P   Q

This graph will help you track your reading progress. Your teacher will use Reading A-Z to check your reading level each quarter and you will color the graph to show where you are. This graph is PERSONAL and is not something you will share with friends.

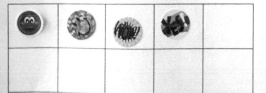

Setting a Student WIG

Now it is time for students to take a turn. Some students will have ideas for WIGs bouncing out of their innovative minds. Others will need help. Identifying a WIG starts with identifying students' greatest challenges, which may be one of the below examples:

PERSONAL GOALS

- I want to be a leader of soccer.
- I want to go to bed earlier at night.
- I want to learn to say the names of all 7 Habits.
- I need to eat healthier.
- I need to do better at getting to school on time.
- I want to do better at listening when the teacher is talking.
- I want to make new friends.
- I want to give a speech at Leadership Day.
- I want to do 10 push-ups.

ACADEMIC GOALS

- I want to increase my stamina in reading.
- I want to learn the times tables to 10.
- I want to turn my homework in on time.
- I want to get a 90 percent or better on my science test.
- I want to learn how to use a calculator.
- I want to learn all 50 sight words for this term.
- I want to mentor other students in spelling.

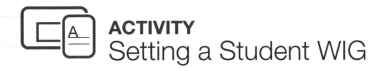

ACTIVITY
Setting a Student WIG

Some students will need a lot of help setting a WIG early on. With very young students, you may need to write the WIG for them or let them draw it in picture form. Some scoreboards will be very simple. With time, students will do it on their own.

Thoughts to consider when setting a WIG with a student include:

- If the class has a WIG, have the student choose a WIG that will contribute to the class WIG.

- Have the student set one academic WIG and one personal WIG. (See sample topics for WIGs on the previous page.)

- Have students set and track WIGs that are similar so that the teacher does not need to track so many types of WIGs.

For students who are able to identify WIGs on their own, ask them such questions as:

- What is the one thing that, if you were to do it more effectively, would help you do better at school?

- What steps could you take (or strategies could you use) to do better at that one thing?

- How might you track how you are doing in implementing those strategies?

- Who would be a good friend or person to check up with you to see how you are doing?

- How will you celebrate when you make improvements in these areas?

Use the worksheet on the following two pages to draft a student WIG.

STUDENT WIG PLANNING WORKSHEET

FOCUS ON THE WILDLY IMPORTANT

What is the "end in mind"?

 Where I am now.

 Where I want to be.

 By when.

ACT ON THE LEAD MEASURES

What one or two strategies or action steps are most important to achieve the WIG?

CREATE A CADENCE OF ACCOUNTABILITY

My Accountability Partner(s) is:

When and where we will meet is:

How I will celebrate is:

KEEP A COMPELLING SCOREBOARD

How will I track my lead measures?

How will I track progress toward my goal?

Leadership Notebooks

A Leadership Notebook is a compact tool for students to gather a sampling of their academic progress, leadership qualities, personal reflections, and best work. While teachers and students should feel comfortable designing the Leadership Notebook in a way that will best meet their needs, a suggested format is to separate the notebooks into five tabs:

- My Self
- My WIGs
- My Learning
- My Leadership
- My Celebrations

Leadership Notebooks

This video overviews the impact of Leadership Notebooks. What do you feel are the benefits Leadership Notebooks can have for:

Students?

Teachers?

Parents?

Making the Leadership Notebook Your Own

It is important that both student and teacher feel ownership for the Leadership Notebooks. Collaborate with students to make them useful and fun. Consider the following tips:

TIPS:

- Students should feel they own their Leadership Notebook. This begins by having them assemble it and somehow participate in the cover design.

- Using thin binders helps to avoid the temptation to make the Leadership Notebook bulky. It is not meant to be a file cabinet for everything a child completes.

- A student leadership role can be created for students to help assemble and/or distribute sections of the Leadership Notebook.

- When kept current, Leadership Notebooks provide the perfect tool for use in Student-Led Conferences and individual accountability sessions. Students are proud to share them.

- Be in them frequently!

Tab 1: My Self

The first tab is a favorite of students. It is where students capture things about themselves, such as their strengths and interests.

Examples of what might be included are:

- A photo of themselves and the class.

- Copies of their personal, class, and school mission statements.

- A summary of the 7 Habits.

- Personal reflections about favorite leaders.

- Highlights of their strengths and hobbies.

While this tabbed section can easily be one of the highlights of the Leadership Notebook, be careful not to turn it into a scrapbook. Four to eight pages is sufficient.

All About Me!

This is me ...

Jason

Things I like ...

I like to eat ...

My family ...
mom and Dad sisters me

Gold Room Code of Cooperation
2014-2015

We greet visitors with a smile and a shake.	
We use kind words with one another.	"Please" "Thank you!" "May I..."
We will clean up after ourselves.	
Be problem solvers.	

Capital Letter Graph   Capital Letters

Our DISTRICT Mission Statement

The mission of the Parkway School District is to ensure that all stud are capable, curious and confident learners who understand and spond to the challenges of an ever-changing world.

Our SCHOOL Mission Statement

Growing Capable Learners... Inspiring Lifetime Leade

Our CLASSROOM Mission Statement

We are a team of curious leaders who will be caring, confident respectful, responsible, and trustworthy. We are hard workers who learn from our mistakes, stay positive, and be successful!

My PERSONAL Mission Statement

I will do my best to help encou
my class to set an exsample
I will also be truthful respectf
and kind to my class and teac

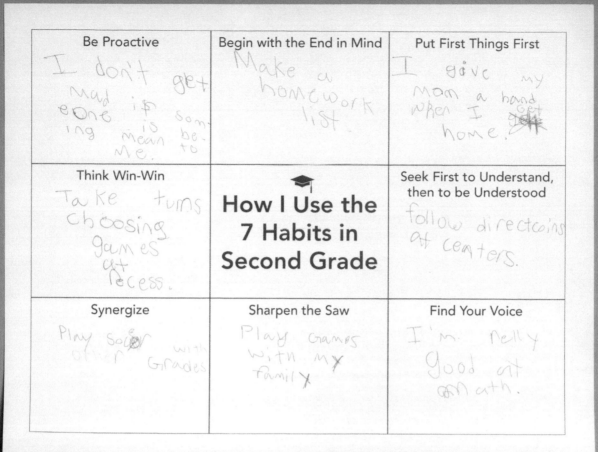

Be Proactive	Begin with the End in Mind	Put First Things First
I don't get mad if eone is som ing mean to me.	Make a homework list.	I gave my mom a hand when I Get home.
Think Win-Win	**How I Use the 7 Habits in Second Grade**	Seek First to Understand, then to be Understood
Take turns choosing games at recess.		follow directcoins at centers.
Synergize	Sharpen the Saw	Find Your Voice
Play socer with other Grades	Play Games with my family	I'm relly good at math.

Greyson
My Vision Board

Annie's
LEADER
Macaroni & Cheese

home
WHERE LIFE HAPPENS

September

I like Nice
Candy Color
Life
COOL
Mr. Happy

© Franklin Covey

Fantastic Great

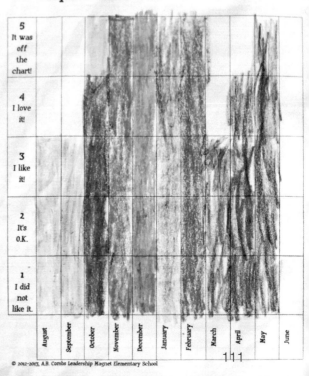

My Enthusiasm for Third Grade

	August	September	October	November	December	January	February	March	April	May	June
5 It was off the chart!											
4 I love it!											
3 I like it!											
2 It's O.K.											
1 I did not like it.											

111

All About My School

School Name: Las Lomas Elementry School

School Mascot: Lions

School Colors: Gold Pur

My school is special because: It is a great school and has nice teachers

Seven Habits "1" Graph

How well did you practice the 7 Habits in the 1st quarter of this school year? Consider the explanation of the 7 Habits below. These are based on the GA Keys instruction strand standards. Use a crayon or marker to create a bar graph that represents how often you practiced this habit.

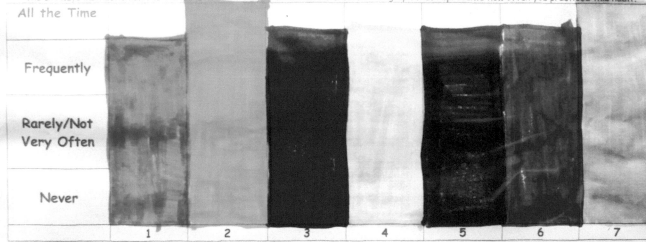

All the Time						
Frequently						
Rarely/Not Very Often						
Never						
1	2	3	4	5	6	7

1. <u>Be Proactive</u>: I had a "Can Do" attitude. I did the right thing without being asked, even if nobody was looking. Color green.
2. <u>Begin with the End in Mind</u>: I planned ahead and set goals. Color blue.
3. <u>Put First Things First</u>: I spent my time on things that are most important. I planned well and stayed organized. Color red.
4. <u>Think Win-Win</u>: I wanted everyone to be a success. It made me happy to see other people happy. Color yellow.
5. <u>Seek first to understand, then to be understood</u>: I listened to other people's ideas and feelings. Color black.
6. <u>Synergize</u>: I valued other people's strengths and learned from them. I got along well with others, even people who are different from me. Color orange.
7. <u>Sharpen the Saw</u>: I took care of my body by eating right, exercising, and getting sleep. Color pink.

Tab 2: My WIGs

This is the tab behind which students record and track their Wildly Important Goals (WIGs). Only one to three WIGs are tracked by students at any time. The WIGs kept here most often link to areas of personal leadership and academics.

Examples of what might be included are:

Personal-Leadership WIGs

- Attendance/tardies

- On-time assignments

- Classroom behavior

- Physical fitness

Academic WIGs

- Reading progress

- Math progress

- Other academic subject areas

I will read _____ books.	I will listen to my teacher.	I will learn all my letters.	I will count to 50.	I will play nicely at recess.
I will finish my work on time.	I will write my own name.	I will work nicely with others.	I will keep my desk neat.	I will share with my friends.
I will cut along the lines.	I will color neatly.	I will write neatly.	I will learn to use a computer.	I will do all my homework.
I will pack up quickly and quietly.	I will raise my hand.	I will sit properly in my seat.	I will sit nicely on the rug.	I will use walking feet.

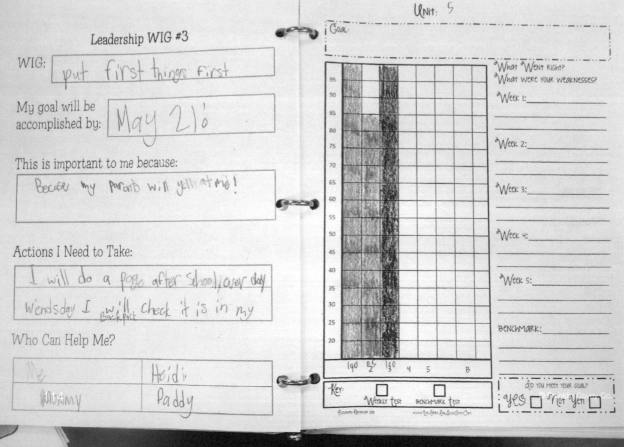

Leadership WIG #3

WIG: put first things first

My goal will be accomplished by: May 21'o

This is important to me because:
Becoee my parents will yell at me!

Actions I Need to Take:
I will do a page after school every day
Wendsday I will check it is in my Backpack

Who Can Help Me?

| Me | Heidi |
| Mummy | Paddy |

Unit: 5

Goal:

95
90
85
80
75
70
65
60
55
50
45
40
35
30
25
20

1 90 85 1 30 4 5 B

What Went Right?
What Were Your Weaknesses?

Week 1: _____
Week 2: _____
Week 3: _____
Week 4: _____
Week 5: _____

BENCHMARK: _____

Key: ☐ Weekly test   ☐ Benchmark test

Did you meet your goal?
Yes ☐   Not yet ☐

Worksheet 1 (Addilyn)

Name: Addilyn   Date: _____

Begin with the End in Mind -- My Wildly Important Goals

My Academic W.I.G. (Be Specific. What positive goal would you like to happen?)

I will get 100% on my spelling tests.

I will achieve my goal by Friday, October 30, 2015.

Action Step (How I will achieve my goal/effort.)

1. I will practice my spelling words for 20 minutes a day.

October Daily W.I.G. Tracker

Sunday	Monday	Tuesday	Wednesday	Thursday	Friday	Saturday	Effort Ratio
				1	2	3	2.2
4	5	6 ✓	7 ✓	8 ✓	9 ✓	10	4.5
11 ✗	12 ✗	13	14	15 ✓	16 No School	17	4.5
18 No School	19 No School	20	21 ✓	22 ✓	23	24	3.4
25 ✓	26	27 ✓	28 ✓	29 ✗	30 ✓	31 Halloween	5.5

Total: 18/20

Worksheet 2 (Brennan)

Name: Brennan   Date: 9-29-15

Begin with the End in Mind—My Wildly Important Goals

My Academic W.I.G. (Be specific. What positive goal would you like to happen?)

I will follow all the school rules.

I will achieve my goal by Friday, October 30, 2015.

ACTION STEP (How I will achieve my goal/effort.)

1. I will not get warnings.

Month of October (Daily WIG Tracker)

Sunday	Monday	Tuesday	Wednesday	Thursday	Friday	Saturday	Effort Ratio
				1 ✓	2 ✓	3	2.2
4	5 ✓	6	7 ✓	8 ✓	9 ✓	10	5.5
11	12 ✓	13	14	15 ✓	16 NO SCHOOL	17	4.4
18	19 NO SCHOOL Professional Develop.	20 ✓	21 ✓	22 ✓	23 ✓	24	4.4
25	26 ✓	27	28 ✗	29 ✓	30 ✓	31 Halloween	3.4

Total: 8/12

My Goals

Week of: _____

Goals						
look at people when I talk.	🙂					
I wait for my turn to talk.	🙂					
I pick the clothes I wear.	☹️					
I play with my friends.	🙂					
I can wash my hands and face.	🙂					

Name __Brennan__ Date __9-29-15__

Begin with the End in Mind—My Wildly Important Goals

My Academic W.I.G. (Be specific. What positive goal would you like to happen?)

I will __follow all the school__
__rules.__

I will achieve my goal by Friday, October 30, 2015.

ACTION STEP (How I will achieve my goal/effort.)

1. __I will not get__
__warnings.__

Month of October (Daily WIG Tracker)

Sunday	Monday	Tuesday	Wednesday	Thursday	Friday	Saturday	Effort Ratio
				1 ✓	2 ✓	3	3⁄2
4	5 ✓	6 ✓	7 ✓	8 ✓	9 ✓	10	5⁄5
11	12 ✓	13	14	15	16 NO SCHOOL ice sundae!	17	4⁄4
18	19 NO SCHOOL Professional Develop.	20 ✓	21 ✓	22 ✓	23 ✓	24	4⁄4
25	26 ✓	27 ✗	28 ✓	29 ✓	30 ✓	31 Halloween	3⁄4

Total: __19⁄20__

Academic WIG Planner

I will go from __11__ reading points
to __17__ reading points
by __June 2015__

Action Steps

1. Read to Self

2. Guided Reading

3. Practice Letterland
words and sight words

Who can help me achieve my WIG?

⭐Ms. Randle ⭐Mrs. Adams ⭐ Mom

Signed __Greyson Bamonte__
Date __10-15-2014__

© Franklin Covey Co.

Tab 3: My Learning

This tab houses other indicators of progress that are important but not considered WIGs. In fact, things kept behind this tab may not be goals at all, but simply data showing progress in various subject or behavior areas.

Examples of what might be included are:

- A chart tracking spelling scores.

- A checklist showing progress on a science project.

- A fun chart showing math facts learned.

- Progress indicators for special classes (e.g., music, art, physical education).

- Any item suggested for the WIGs tab that is not considered by the teacher or student to be a WIG.

Limit it to 10 items or less. Sometimes less is more.

2nd Grade Sight Words

1st Q= red
2nd Q= orange
3rd Q= yellow
4th Q= green

3rd Quarter	I can read this word with fluency.	I can spell this word.
again		
another		
ask		
because		
change		
different		
does		
even		
hand		
kind		
land		
large		
men		
move		
must		
need		
off		
picture		
read		
such		
together		
try		
turn		
well		
why		

4th Quarter	I can read this word with fluency.	I can spell this word.
air		
always		
animal		
answer		
ask		
end		
found		
learn		
letter		
mean		
mother		
off		
page		
picture		
please		
point		
round		
should		
still		
think		
through		
under		
which		
world		
year		

My Fitness Goal
"Begin With the End in Mind"

Choose one goal you would like to set for yourself in PE. If you would like to choose your own, check the "other" and fill in your goal.

	I will improve my running.
	I will improve my curl ups.
	I will improve my push-up
X	I will improve my flexibility.
	Other:

Why did you choose this goal?
Because I'm not very flexable.

Alphabet Lowercase Names

Color up the bar as you learn the letter names! Kids can also mark the ones the

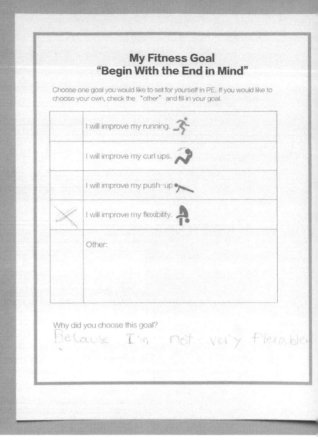

| 26 |
| 25 |
| 24 |
| 23 |
| 22 |
| 21 |
| 20 |
| 19 |
| 18 |
| 17 |
| 16 |
| 15 |
| 14 |
| 13 |
| 12 |
| 11 |
| 10 |
| 9 |
| 8 |
| 7 |
| 6 |
| 5 |
| 4 |
| 3 |

a b c d
f g h i j
l m n o
q r s t
v w x y

© Franklin Covey Co.

Multiplication Facts

Name ~~Trey~~ Logan

 | × 8

 | × 6,7,8

× 4 | × 9

× 5 | × 10

× 3,4,5 | × 11

× 6 | × 12

× 7 | × 9,10,11,12

Oral Reading Fluency Goals

Story	Words Per Minute	Accuracy	Retell	Goal for Next Reading
	Beginning: 70 Middle: 86 End: 100	Beginning: 95% Middle: 96% End: 97%	Beginning: 20 Middle: 26 End: 30	
DIBELS 1	137	99%	59	137
DIBELS 2	135	100%	42	138
DIBELS 3	144	100%	41	146
DIBELS 4	165	99%	76	167
DIBELS 5	142	99%	51	147
DIBELS 6				
DIBELS 7				
DIBELS 8				
DIBELS 9				
DIBELS 10				
DIBELS 11				
DIBELS 12				

My Weeks of Positive Behavior

(Each number colored is one week of proactive choices with no recess det...

1	2	3	4	5
7	8	9	10	11
13	14	15	16	17
19	20	21	22	23
25	26	27	28	29
31	32	33	34	35

MY WORD STUDY ASSESSMENT DATA

QTR. 3

The difference between the right word and the almost right word is the difference between lightning and a lightning bug.
Mark Twain

(bar chart: 100%, 90%, 80%, 70%, 60%, 50%, 40%, 30%, 20%, 10%, 0%)
Bars labeled: 2/22/13, 3/11/13

Reflection

What does your data tell you about your word study performance?

This data tells me that I have worked hard and succeeded in spelling.

What will you continue to do? What will you change?

I will continue to keep up the effort and change how I learn.

120

MY SCIENCE ASSESSMENT D

QTR. 3

SCIENCE IS A WAY OF THINKING MUCH MORE THAN IT IS A BODY OF KNOWLED...
CARL SAGAN

(bar chart: 100%, 90%, 80%, 70%, 60%, 50%, 40%, 30%, 20%, 10%, 0%)
Bars labeled: 2/8/13 science check up, 2/15/13 checkup, 3/6/13 science check up, science checkup

Reflection   2/22/13 checkup

What does your data tell you about your science performance?

This data tells me that my science performance has helped me to learn more science.

What will you continue to do? What will you change?

I will continue to work hard and get b... scores.

Tab 4: My Leadership

This tab captures a student's experiences and learning as a leader. For young ages, it may be a simple checklist of roles they have filled. For older ages, it may be more of a leadership journal where they record weekly reflections on what they have enjoyed and learned about leadership.

Examples of what might be included are:

- A list of leadership roles fulfilled.

- A weekly journal of reflections on how the student was a leader that week.

- A collection of favorite quotes on leadership.

- Insights from a student's Accountability Partner on things the student did well or could enhance.

LEADERSHIP

My Leadership Roles

1. Bathroom Leader	2. Cafeteria Leader
3. Playground Leader	4. Mail Leader
5. Folder Leader	6. Lunch Box Leader
7.	8.
9.	10.
11.	12.

Emma

Art Crafting Leadership Group Reflection

Our mission statement is: The Art Crafting leaders ar Students who synergize and sharpen the saw ny creatively promoting leadership with origi works of art.

The habit I demonstrate is ThinK win+win bec we all work together and we take turns, beause one time I was just painting the flowe and one girl was left out so me and her did together.

Through this leadership role, I have learned to synergize and also sharpen the saw wit Painting it was fun to synergize and sharpen the saw at the same time.

Leadership Role Reflection

My Leadership Role This Week
_____
_____
_____
_____

What kind of job did I do?

Would I do the job again?

122

Leadership Roles

1. Line Leader
2. Teacher Helper
3. School Store
4. Greeter for Grandparents Day
5. Attendance Helper
6. Eraser Helper
7. Vice President for Lighthouse Tea
8. Computer Helper
9. Girl Bathroom Monitor
10. Binder Helper
11. Data Wall

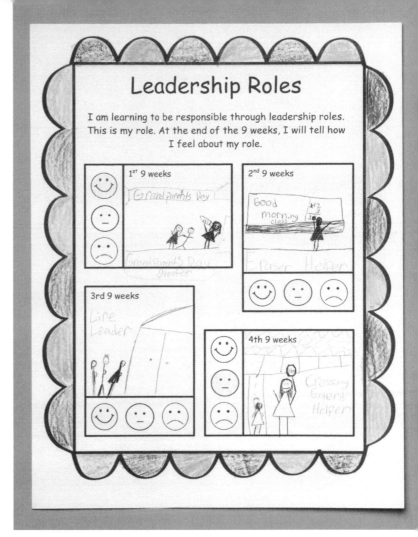

Accountability Partner Reflection Sheet

Date:	Reflection:
Date: January Partner Name: ella	Good, read fluentcy and good timing
Date: febuary Partner Name: ella	We needed more and better timing the words were not on our range.
Date: march Partner Name: ella	great month nice quick turns, good fluency
Date: april Partner Name: ella	Rading to a good time and I could comprehend what I read
Date: 	Reflection:

123

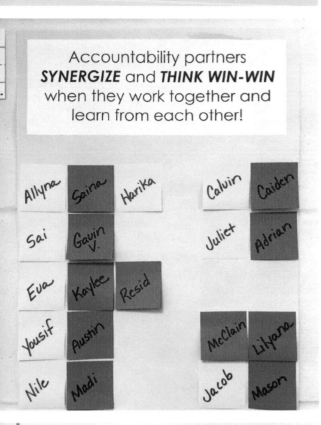

Accountability partners **SYNERGIZE** and **THINK WIN-WIN** when they work together and learn from each other!

Allyna Saina Harika   Calvin Caiden
Sai Gavin V.   Juliet Adrian
Eva Kaylee Resid
Yousif Austin   McClain Lilyana
Nile Madi   Jacob Mason

How to be an EXCELLENT Accountability Partne[r]

Using synergy to analyze and monitor progress on goals and action st[eps] in order to ensure success.

Behavior	Looks Like	Sounds Like
Active Listening	• Eyes on your partner as they share • Hands empty and still • Attentive posture • Focused mind on partner's Leadership Notebook	• Mainly partne[r] voice • Positive respo[nse] goals and prog[ress] • Conversation [with] • One voice at a [time]
Encourage	• Plan your comments before speaking • Make eye contact when you are speaking	• Use positive w[ords] • Be specific and explain your comments
Question	• Plan your questions before asking • Make eye contact when you are speaking	• Ask questions positive way • Focus question[s] Leadership Notebook
Reflect	• Working together (think win-win and synergy) • Focused on thoughts and ideas	• Discussion foc[used] on today's mee[ting] • One voice at a [time] but both contr[ibute] to reflection

Ask Yourself:

Did you...
- synergize to meet the expectations of the time with your accountability p[artner]
- seek first to understand (listen first) when discussing goals and progress[?]
- make this time a win-win for you and your partner by following the expe[ctations?]

Enzo

Enzo

My Accountability Partner

My partner is in ___Mrs. Campbell___'s class.

___Enzo___ is in ___1st___ grade.

My partner's favorite thing about school is

___lunch___.

124

Tab 5: My Celebrations

The greatest reward of progress is the feeling of progress. Progress comes in many forms: improving academically, developing a new talent, or helping another person progress. This tab is where such magic is celebrated.

Examples of what might be included are:

- A test representing a personal best.

- A certificate, ribbon, or sticker earned.

- Photographs of team accomplishments.

- Notes of praise or gratitude.

- Non-school accomplishments (e.g., earning a yellow belt in karate).

- Achieved WIGs.

Students love extrinsic rewards. But the rewards that last and truly motivate are intrinsic. When using extrinsic rewards, always pair them with an intrinsic reward, such as a compliment about a character trait the student exhibited when achieving a goal.

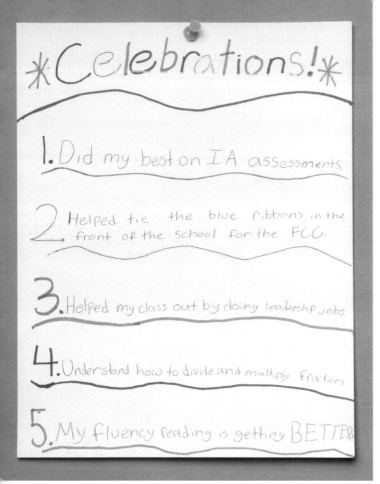

Celebrations!

1. Did my best on I A assessments.

2. Helped tie the blue ribbons in the front of the school for the FCC.

3. Helped my class out by doing leadership jobs

4. Understand how to divide and multiply fractions

5. My fluency reading is getting BETTER

WORLD'S
FRIENDLIEST

This certificate is awarded to:

Tulasi Velga

in recognition of

her ability to be a friend to everyone!

Signature   Date

I met my goal...

at summer izing

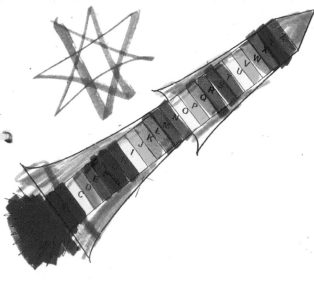

AOfo _____ **is**

ROCKETING towards being a
master of addition facts!

Color in each letter when you
pass its 2 minute timing.

My Accomplishments, Celebrations, and Contributions

A good Life is a collection of happy moments.

❧ 1st Nine Weeks

❧ 2nd Nine Weeks

_____
_____
_____
_____
_____

_____
_____
_____
_____
_____

❧ 3rd Nine Weeks

❧ 4th Nine Weeks

_____
_____
_____
_____
_____

_____
_____
_____
_____
_____

Jobs:

Job is _____ I (liked / did not like) this job, because
_____

Job is _____ I (liked / did not like) this job, because
_____

Job is _____ I (liked / did not like) this job, because
_____

Job is _____ I (liked / did not like) this job, because

6 Unit Test   Name _____   ⑮ ⑤

Toys at the Toy Store

Balls	🔵🔵🔵🔵🔵🔵
Bears	🧸🧸🧸🧸🧸🧸🧸
Cars	🚗🚗🚗

Use the graph to answer the questions below.

1. Are there more balls or cars? ball ✓
2. Are there fewer cars or bears? cars ✓
3. The store has the most of which toy? bears

4. Make a picture graph about the shapes.

🟥⬛⬛🟥⬛🟥🔴🔴⬛🔴🔴⬛🔴

Circles							
Rectangles							

5. Complete the sentences. Ring the word **more** or **fewer**.

There are [2] **more** ~~fewer~~ rectangles than circles.

There are [2] more ~~fewer~~ circles than rectangles.

127

UNIT 6

Congratulations,
Mrs. Estes' Kindergarten
class has turned in all
their library books!!
Keep up the good work!!
Week22

Congratulations,
Mrs. Estes' Kindergarten
class has turned in all
their library books!!
Keep up the good work!!
Week24

ATTENDANCE

Class of the Week

MONDAY ★ WEDNESDAY FRIDAY

TUESDAY THURSDAY

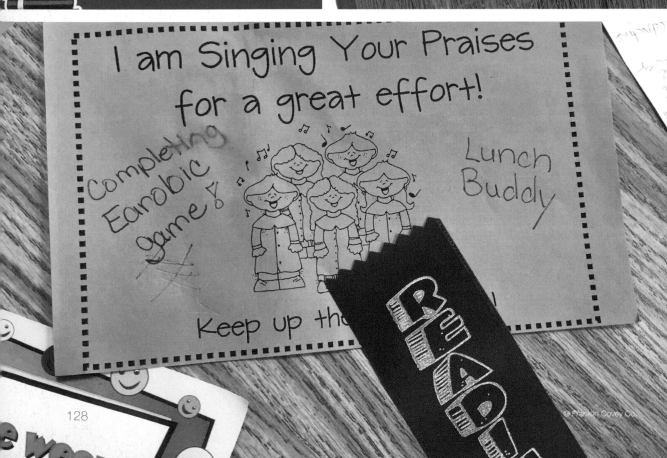

I am Singing Your Praises
for a great effort!

Completing
Earobic
game!

Lunch
Buddy

Keep up the

© Franklin Covey Co.

We completed another Village Goal!!!

Goal: To show responsibility by taking better care of our belongings in the locker room

Goal set on December 8, 2014

Goal met on February 10, 2015

Goal success celebrated March 2, 2015

Celebrated by enjoying the movie Big Hero 6 with popcorn and juice boxes!!

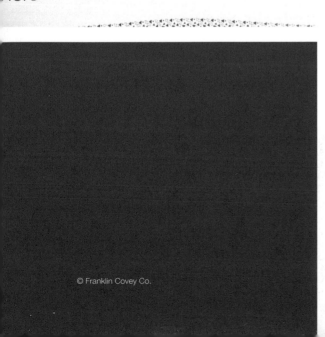

I met my goal of Keyboarding on the cunputere

Name Reogan G

Date 8-2

129

ACTIVITY
Planning Your Leadership Notebook

Plan your Leadership Notebook. What types of things will you put in each section?

Front Cover: What will the front cover look like? Who will design it?

Tab 1: My Self

Tab 2: My WIGs

Tab 3: My Learning

Tab 4: My Leadership

Tab 5: My Celebrations

Student-Led Conferences

Often schools hold parent-teacher conferences to update parents on how well students are progressing. With *The Leader in Me*, the students take ownership for leading the discussion. Such discussions can be held with parents in formal settings a few times a year, or they can be held in more casual settings with students sharing their progress with other students or mentors throughout the school year.

 **VIDEO**

Student-Led Conferences

What in this video do you see as benefits of Student-Led Conferences:

For students?

For parents?

For teachers?

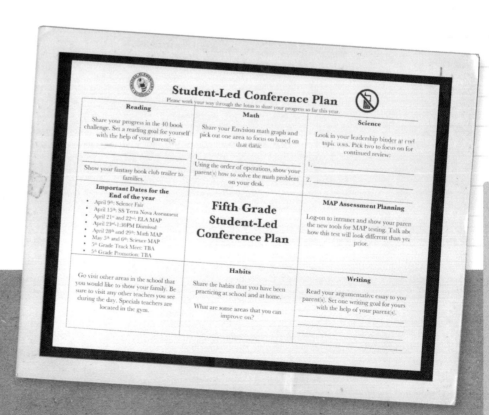

STUDENT-LED CONFERENCE (SAMPLE AGENDA)

INTRODUCE your parents or (guests) to your teacher.

FIND your Leadership Notebook and a quiet place to sit.

SHARE important items in each tab of your Leadership Notebook.

FOCUS on areas of strength and on one or two areas you are trying to improve.

ASK your parents (or guests) for suggestions to help.

INVITE your teacher to share additional information.

SHOW appreciation for everyone's support and listening.

END quietly so that others are not interrupted.

Student-Led Conference Checklist

✓ 1. Take your parent(s) to a conference area around the school.

✓ 2. Share your data notebook.

✓ 3. Discuss your strengths. Ask your parents to tell you what they think your strengths are.

✓ 4. Talk about what you need to work on for 4th grade. Ask your parents what they think you should work on.

✓ 5. Finish your lunch and say good-bye. Thank your parent(s) for coming and give them a big hug!

Dear Family:

To help you better understand what is going on with your child's learning this year, we are holding a different type of parent-teacher conference. Tuesday, November 8, we will hold a Student-Led Conference.

Your student will lead the conference and explain to you what he or she has been accomplishing around academic and personal goals. Your child has been collecting data throughout the year and is prepared to present these achievements during the first 10–15 minutes of the conference. The second half of the conference will be with your child's classroom teacher.

What you can expect:

1. You and your child will have time to go though his or her portfolio of work.

2. You and your child will meet with the teacher to discuss your child's learning and performance.

3. You and the teacher will discuss growth opportunities for your child.

Students are preparing hard for this conference, so please be sure to attend. It is their chance to show you all the growth they have accomplished so far this year. I look forward to seeing everyone.

Sincerely,

Amy Cardona

Principal

ACTIVITY
Planning a Student-Led Conference

In a small team, plan out what you might do with a Student-Led Conference, whether it be formal or informal.

When will the Student-Led Conference be held?

To whom will students present their progress?

___ Parent(s)/guardian(s)

___ A peer student

___ A student mentor

___ A staff member or guest

What pre-work needs to be completed prior to the conference?

What agenda or flow will the student follow?

What follow-up will happen afterward?

Student WIG Summary

	PLAN (Mental Creation)	**EXECUTE** (Physical Creation)
Focus on the Wildly Important	• Involve students in identifying the single most leveraged task that will impact his or her effectiveness. • Determine where he or she is (X). • Establish where he or she wants to be (Y). • Set a *when*. • Clarify *why* the WIG is important.	• Post the WIG in a visible place (e.g., Leadership Notebook) where the student will see it on a regular basis. • Refer to the WIG and the why often.
Act on the Lead Measures	• Work with the student to identify strategies or action steps that will lead to the achievement of the student's WIG. • Select the two or three most leveraged strategies or actions that will lead the student to achieving the WIG. • Identify the lead measures. • Create a plan for addressing the lead measures.	• Encourage the student to act on the lead measures. • Give the student a consistent time to work on lead measures. • Remind the student to maintain her or his "whirlwind." • Help the student say no to unimportant tasks.
Keep a Compelling Scoreboard	• Include both lead measures and lag measures in the student's scoreboard. • Set goal lines when appropriate. • Meet the five-second rule.	• Post the scoreboard in a visible place (e.g., Leadership Notebook). • Update the scoreboard weekly, if not more often.
Create a Cadence of Accountability	• Identify an Accountability Partner for the student. • Set weekly time (short and undivided) for holding one-on-one WIG Sessions with the student.	• Meet at a designated time, as well as special times like Student-Led Conferences. • Have the student report on commitments. • Update and review the scoreboard. • Make new commitments, including clearing the path. • Adjust as needed. (Is the goal still realistic? Is the meeting time working? Do we have the right lead measures? etc.) • Celebrate!

Notes

Notes

Wrapping Up

- Putting It All Together
- Designing an Implementation Plan

Putting It All Together

In concluding *Aligning Academics*, it is helpful to review the bigger picture and see how leadership, culture, and academics integrate with each other to impact what happens at school. In doing so, it becomes clear that all three components impact each other. To try to address academic matters, for example, will be very difficult and discouraging if the culture of the school is not conducive to learning. Likewise, it will be very unlikely for a student to do well, both in school and in life, if he or she does not have some of the basic skills for leading self and working with others. The challenges are all integrated and need to be seen as a whole.

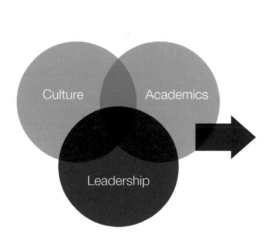

To enable people to be more:

- Independent.
- Interdependent.
- Able to make a meaningful contribution.

"By picking a good team, by picking members we knew would work, by expecting certain things out of people, and by planning in advance…the success of the expedition was decided way in advance of Nepal."

P. V. SCATURRO, EVEREST TEAM LEADER

VIDEO
Jalen

Identify how you think leadership, culture, and academics each impacted Jalen's performance at school. Do you think if the school had only focused on one area that Jalen would have progressed as much as he did?

Leadership

Culture

Academics

Designing an Implementation Plan

When creating an implementation plan, take into consideration all three challenges—leadership, culture, and academics. Focus on your own role, not on the school as a whole.

Leadership and Culture. For implementation ideas relative to leadership and culture, refer back to previous activities and discussions, particularly on pages 4–13 and the Appendix.

Academics. For implementation ideas regarding personal, team (class), and student WIGs, including academics, consider making a rollout plan similar to the following:

WEEK 1	WEEK 2	WEEK 4	WEEK 6	BEYOND
Post your personal WIG and begin modeling the process for students.	Have the class set a WIG for how they will be leaders or improve the culture of the school. Have them place it in their Leadership Notebook and begin the 4DX® process of tracking, scoreboarding, and being accountable.	Assess students' reading skills, identify a class reading WIG based on the results, and create a scoreboard. Use the 4DX process.	Once students understand how the class reading WIG works, help them set a personal reading WIG that will contribute to the class WIG.	Introduce additional WIGs (short-term or long-term) as needed and as students are ready.

Below is a sample implementation plan for a year. Notice how items are spread out over the year. Remember, "Balance is best."

SAMPLE: THINGS TO CONSIDER IN AN IMPLEMENTATION CHECKLIST

BEFORE SCHOOL	☐ Post my personal WIG in the classroom for students to see.
	☐ Plan out and gather materials for Leadership Notebooks.
TERM 1	Spend much of first two weeks building the culture of the class, including:
	☐ Review all 7 Habits with students. Have students teach the habits.
	☐ Get students to identify and apply for leadership roles.
	☐ Have students create 7 Habits displays for the classroom.
	☐ Create a class mission statement and "Code of Cooperation."
	☐ Have students begin assembling Leadership Notebooks.
	☐ Share my personal WIG with students and have them be my Accountability Partners.
	☐ Assess students' reading ability and set a classroom reading WIG. Create a scoreboard.
	☐ Help students set individual reading WIGs, and set time for WIG Sessions.
TERM 2	☐ Celebrate milestones for WIG achievement for Term 1. Have students place their best work in their Leadership Notebook.
	☐ Hold a family 7 Habits skit night.
	☐ Prepare students for the first round of Student-Led Conferences.
TERM 3	☐ Celebrate milestones for WIG achievement for Term 2. Have students place their best work in their Leadership Notebook.
	☐ Rotate classroom leadership roles.
	☐ Prepare a class skit for Leadership Day.
	☐ Do a classroom WIG for the school fund-raiser.
TERM 4	☐ Celebrate milestones for WIG achievement for Term 3. Have students place their best work in their Leadership Notebook.
	☐ Hold the wax museum fair where students portray historical leaders.
	☐ Meet with the grade-level team to debrief the year.

ACTIVITY
Creating an Implementation Plan

In the space below, or on another tool, draft an implementation plan for taking *The Leader in Me* to a higher level in your role.

BEFORE SCHOOL	
TERM 1	Tip: Spend much of the first two weeks building the culture of the class.
TERM 2	

TERM 3	
TERM 4	

Did you remember these "Big Rocks"?

- Post and model a personal WIG.

- Help students write and track an individual WIG.

- Organize Leadership Notebooks.

- Set and track a class academic WIG.

- Set and track a student academic WIG that aligns to the class WIG.

Notes

Notes

Notes

Appendix

- ## Self-Assessing the 7 Habits

The 7 Habits Self-Assessment

One way to improve your effectiveness as a leader is to reflect on the 7 Habits and identify one specific aspect you can improve upon. Or in other words, identify the one thing that, if improved upon, will have the greatest impact on your effectiveness as a leader.

EITHER INDIVIDUALLY OR WITH A PARTNER, TAKE THE FOLLOWING STEPS:

STEP 1. Review the 7 Habits on the next pages.

STEP 2. Assess how you are doing relative to each habit using the tools on pages 157–160.

STEP 3. Identify "the one thing" based on your assessment that, if improved, would have the greatest impact on your personal effectiveness.

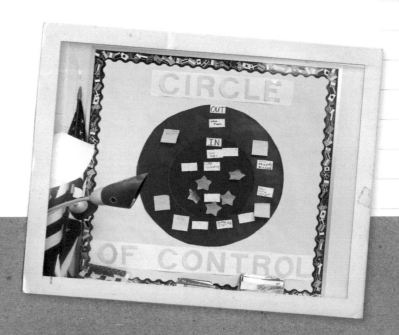

Habit 1:
BE PROACTIVE

	Never			Sometimes				Usually		
	1	2	3	4	5	6	7	8	9	10

I take initiative to get things done.

I maintain self-control, even in difficult or emotional circumstances.

I focus on things I can do something about rather than on things beyond my control.

I accept responsibility for my actions rather than making excuses.

What is the one thing I can do to live Habit 1 at a higher level?

_____

_____

Habit 2:
BEGIN WITH THE END IN MIND

	Never			Sometimes				Usually		
	1	2	3	4	5	6	7	8	9	10

I begin projects with a clear understanding of the desired outcomes.

I have a sense of direction in my life.

I use my Personal Mission Statement to make decisions.

I make time to reconnect with my vision often. I have clear goals.

What is the one thing I can do to live Habit 2 at a higher level?

_____

_____

APPENDIX

Habit 3:
PUT FIRST THINGS FIRST

	Never			Sometimes				Usually		
	1	2	3	4	5	6	7	8	9	10

I say no to unimportant requests.

I plan carefully so that I can avoid falling into crisis mode.

I achieve my top two or three most important tasks each week.

I prioritize by scheduling time for the things that matter most.

What is the one thing I can do to live Habit 3 at a higher level?

_____

_____

Habit 4:
THINK WIN-WIN

	Never			Sometimes				Usually		
	1	2	3	4	5	6	7	8	9	10

I make regular, sincere deposits in the Emotional Bank Accounts of others.

I have the courage to say no when appropriate.

I work to find win-win solutions.

I take time to understand what a win is for others.

What is the one thing I can do to live Habit 4 at a higher level?

_____

_____

Habit 5:
SEEK FIRST TO UNDERSTAND, THEN TO BE UNDERSTOOD

	Never				Sometimes				Usually	
	1	2	3	4	5	6	7	8	9	10

I listen without interrupting.

I attempt to understand problems before attempting to solve them.

I present my ideas clearly and concisely.

I try to see things from the other person's point of view, not just my own.

What is the one thing I can do to live Habit 5 at a higher level?

_____

_____

Habit 6:
SYNERGIZE

	Never				Sometimes				Usually	
	1	2	3	4	5	6	7	8	9	10

I seek out the strengths of others to get things done.

I am open-minded to try new ideas.

I value the differences in people.

I seek 3rd Alternatives when solving problems.

What is the one thing I can do to live Habit 6 at a higher level?

_____

_____

	Never			Sometimes				Usually		
	1	2	3	4	5	6	7	8	9	10

Habit 7:
SHARPEN THE SAW

I take time to find enjoyment and
meaning in life.

I care for my physical well-being.

I am a constant learner.

I have a strong network of friends
and co-workers.

What is the one thing I can do to live Habit 7 at a higher level?

_____

_____

- -

WHAT IS YOUR ONE THING?
Look back at your self-assessment. What is the one thing that, if you
were to improve upon it, would have the greatest impact on your
personal effectiveness?